Bucky Told Me
to Put the Stick in the Door

Bucky Told Me
to Put the Stick in the Door

✦

...And Other White Lies to Live By

Carl F. Cusato

iUniverse, Inc.
New York Lincoln Shanghai

Bucky Told Me to Put the Stick in the Door
...And Other White Lies to Live By

iUniverse books may be ordered through booksellers or by contacting:

iUniverse
2021 Pine Lake Road, Suite 100
Lincoln, NE 68512
www.iuniverse.com
1-800-Authors (1-800-288-4677)

ISBN-13: 978-0-595-38960-5 (pbk)
ISBN-13: 978-0-595-84069-4 (cloth)
ISBN-13: 978-0-595-83344-3 (ebk)
ISBN-10: 0-595-38960-0 (pbk)
ISBN-10: 0-595-84069-8 (cloth)
ISBN-10: 0-595-83344-6 (ebk)

Printed in the United States of America

About the Subtitle

This book has a subtitle to protect the author in the event the book is selected by Ophra's Book Club, or any other nationally recognized book recommending organization who might be concerned about it's accuracy. The author, to be safe, is in advance, suggesting that the story is one big lie. If investigators subsequently discover it is not a lie but is the truth, the author, in advance, agrees to appear on national TV to confess without immunity to all transgressions.

To my friend,
Patrick Cunningham,
For his editorial eye, support and encouragement

To my wife,
Robin,
For her patience and understanding

To my children,
Damon and Ashley,
For their sense of humor

Contents

Prologue

Bucky

Four of us stood in the front of the classroom—heads bowed and hands clasped behind our backs as if the MP had just ordered, "Prisoners, parade rest." Bucky, Pete, Billy G, and I, the cream of the fifth grade at St. James Institute—a Catholic parish school run by the Sisters of Saint Joseph—had been nabbed!

Father Benson, the parish priest who towered over us with his 6-foot-4-inch frame, was leading the interrogation. Sister Dolorata, the school principal, stood next to him exuding the warmth of Torquemada, the famous Spanish inquisitor.

For some bizarre reason, we thought it would be a cool idea to break into the school after hours. We didn't want to steal anything or do any damage. We just wanted to see if we could do it.

It was Lent, and we were required to go to church every morning before school—and Lent was a big pain in the ass. We had to get up extra early in the freezing cold to go to the seven o'clock Mass. After Mass, they'd walk us to the auditorium in the basement of the school, and there they would feed us hot chocolate or milk and, once in a while, Freihofer's Hot Cross Buns.

I don't remember how the idea started or why, but it had to be done, and we were possessed. We even planned the details. I thought we should unlock a window. Pete wanted to put scotch tape on the front door lock, and Billy G was for climbing through the bathroom window.

Bucky said, "Just put a stick in the back door."

To be safe, we did all four. It was March, and it got dark about five. I told my mother I'd be late because of choir practice. About 4:15 PM we walked back to the school and eyed our mission. We tried the front door, but someone had removed the tape. We checked the window, but it was locked—even the bathroom window was closed and locked.

Discouraged, but not ready to quit, we crept around to the back and tried the door. To our surprise, it opened. The stick had been in the door all day and nobody noticed. We crept down the back stairs into the auditorium. We stared into the large room with its polished hardwood floors and suddenly realized that we hadn't planned to do anything.

We looked at each other dumbly and thought, *Okay, we broke into the school! Now what?*

Spontaneously, we started running around the auditorium. We took off our shoes, ran, and slid on the polished floors. Sounds pretty stupid, but it was exciting.

Pete thought it would be cool to write something on the blackboard.

He wrote, "Happy Lent, yours truly, Pontius Pilate!" Not very clever, even for an eleven-year-old.

We slipped into the kitchen and there, sitting on the table, was a big stack of boxes filled with Freihofer's Hot Cross Buns.

Freihofer's Hot Cross Buns were special. Instead of the white frosting in the shape of a cross, like common hot cross buns, they had a cinnamon and sugar topping with cinnamon and raisins inside. They were the best. We each took a box, sat on the floor in the auditorium, and stuffed our faces.

It was getting really dark, so we decided to leave. Just as we were about to get up, the lights flashed on, and a deep voice roared, "Hey, you kids, what are you doing in here?"

Like startled deer, we froze. It was McFarland, the janitor.

We screamed and threw the boxes into in the air. We grabbed our shoes, ran up the stairs, out the door and down St. James Place in Olympic time.

All we could say was, "Holy shit, holy shit."

McFarland was an old man, and we hoped he hadn't seen our faces. Still, we didn't know for sure and were really nervous.

Pete and I were serving Mass the next morning and we were extra nice. We got there early. Big smiles. "Yes, Father, no Father, can we help you, Father?" It was really sickening.

Nothing was said in church or at breakfast. By the time we got to class, we figured that we were safe. That was until Father B, McFarland, and Sister Dolorata walked in. The class rose.

"Good Morning, Father Benson. May we have your blessing?" we asked with the usual singsong greeting.

He gave us his blessing and motioned for everyone to sit.

"Can you pick them out, Mr. McFarland?" This voice of doom rattled the classroom window.

McFarland shuffled up and down the aisle, and then without hesitation, pointed to the four of us.

"Cusato, Connell, Farley, Gorezinsky, front and center," the priest commanded.

We rose and walked to the front of the classroom.

Father B stared at us for what seemed an eternity.

"Well, do you deny it?" he said, looking right at me.

"Are you talking to me, Father?" I said.

"I'm talking now," he grabbed the trap muscle right where the shoulder meets the neck. That was his thing, grab the traps and squeeze!

"Were you gentlemen in the school last night?"

"Last night, Father?"

He began squeezing.

"Okay, okay, aaah…yes, briefly," I said. He released his grip.

"And the rest of you?" He began to pace.

After a long pause, in our singsong sarcastic manner, "Yes, Father," we confessed in unison.

"Do you know that breaking and entering is against the law?

"Yes, Father."

"I could have you arrested. Why did you do it?" he growled.

"Not sure, Father."

The interrogation continued with the good nun, Sister Dolorata, adding her loving comments: "They're nothing but trouble, never amount to anything, and they're sneaks." She was such a delightful woman, and wonderful with children.

"Who wrote on the blackboard?" Father B interrupted.

"I did, Father," Pete replied.

"Was that supposed to be funny?"

"Did you think it was, Father?" Pete asked.

"I did not!"

"Then it wasn't," Pete said.

"How did you get in?" Father said, changing the subject.

"We put a stick in the door," I said.

"Who put the stick in the door?"

The silence was deafening.

"Again," he said impatiently, "who put the stick in the door?"

"Well, I did," I cavalierly responded.

He moved toward me. My adrenalin started pumping. Just as he was about to resume his grip of pain, I blurted out, "But…Bucky told me to do it!"

Bucky's eyes blasted open in surprise.

Something must have hit the good Father's funny bone, because the tension immediately disappeared. I could see him chuckling. He walked over to Sister D and they talked for about a minute.

"All right, do you guys promise never to break into the school like this again?"

"Yes, Father!" sensing that the worst was over.

"All right, here's your punishment. You will write the following two thousand times—<u>neatly</u>: *I will not break into the school ever again,* and submit it to me by Friday. In addition, you will work in the school kitchen cleaning up after morning Mass until the end of Lent; and finally, you each owe the school $1.25 for stealing the buns and…I'll expect a note from your parents letting *me know* that *they know* what *you did.*"

I hate writing anything two thousand times. You can only get twenty-five lines on a page. Twenty-five divided into two thousand is eighty pages! You try to make it interesting like writing five pages of "I," then five pages of "will not"…and so on. No matter how you do it, it *makes* you crazy!

By the way, Bucky didn't talk to me for a week.

1

The Neighborhood

My tale begins in 1955. Ike was president. The Cold War was cooking. The atomic bomb was on everyone's mind. Bomb shelters were built in the basement. Commies were on every corner. The 1955 Chevy was the hippest car ever, or a least it seemed so. Elvis was singing "Heartbreak Hotel" and "Hound Dog." Pompadour haircuts combed back on the side in a ducktail loaded down with hair wax were getting popular. Two-pound shell cordovan shoes with horseshoe taps, spit-shined to a mirror, finished the picture. On TV, we watched the *Honeymooners, Gunsmoke, Wyatt Earp, Ozzie and Harriet,* and old black-and-white cartoons.

I was eleven years old in the fifth grade at St. James Institute, a parish school located about a mile from my home. I lived on Second Avenue in downtown Albany, New York. Well, it was uptown then, but it's downtown now. The real downtown then, with tenement houses, poor people, and Green Street with the canopied whorehouses, was about a mile east.

The houses on the street were mostly two-story railroad flats with 10-foot alleys separating them. A small patch of lawn adorned the front and a gigantic 20- by 30-foot lawn in the back.

The House on Second Ave.

They had un-insulated stand-up attics the length of the house that boiled to 110 degrees in the summer and froze in the winter. I loved the attic. It was like my own private clubhouse. When I was a teenager, my father bought a full-sized pool table from a black family for $50. They were using it as a dining table. We put it in the attic. It was the right size but the wrong quality. It was 8 foot by 4 foot but had a plywood top and cheap felt. The balls were half-sized, and the sticks were warped. Still, it was a pool table, and I loved it. The only problem was, on long shots the balls would drift. In order to make a long shot, you aimed about six inches to the side of the pocket. Even the Hudson brothers, who owned a real table and were sharks, couldn't beat me. I cleaned up. I didn't play for money when I played my little brother. We played for pride. The loser had to get on his knees and yell, "*I am a loser*"—ten times. It did wonders for self-esteem.

The full basements held the coal burning furnaces. It was a real treat when, on rare occasions, we had porterhouse steaks. My dad and I would go down in the basement with these foldable wire racks with long handles. We put the steaks in the racks, seasoned them, locked the rack shut and stuck them right in the fire of the furnace—so much for carcinogenic blackened meat. The smell while it burned was incredible. It permeated the entire house, and the taste was even better.

We lived on the second floor while Uncle Joe and Aunt Vicky lived downstairs. It was, at best, semi-private. Uncle Joe was a good guy whom, when I was little, I tormented regularly. I was a real pain in the ass as a kid. We didn't know about hyperactivity in those days and, thank God, Ritalin wasn't invented.

I would sneak down the back stairs, open the door to the kitchen, and hide in the pantry. Uncle Joe loved to read his newspaper. I crept up to his chair, flicked the paper out of his hands, and ran away. Did it every night. Made him crazy! One Easter, I got a rabbit as a present. I let the rabbit loose in his house, and it shit all over the place. My Aunt Vicky got upset, but Joe never got mad. Except one day a few weeks later, he called for me up the back stairs.

"Carlucci (my family nickname), would you like a nice, big dish of ice cream?"

"Ice cream! Yeah, great, Uncle Joe," I yelled while jumping down the stairs.

On the kitchen table, he had the biggest dish of ice cream I ever saw. It had Hershey syrup, whipped cream, and a cherry.

"You have been such a good boy," he said with a big smile, "I thought I'd do something nice for you."

"I have!" I said innocently.

I sat down and picked up my spoon.

"Wait," Uncle Joe interrupted, "put this on so that you'll keep your shirt clean." He tied a dishcloth around my neck.

As I bent over for my first bite, he grabbed the back of my head and ground it into the ice cream...for a long time. I was so shocked that I began to scream. Ice cream, chocolate syrup, whipped cream were rolling off my face like hot lava sliding down a volcano. Still crying, I jumped up and ran upstairs yelling for my mother. My father and mother were sitting at the kitchen table having coffee.

"Maaaaa, look what Uncle Joe did!" I protested.

Trying to hold back the laughter, my mother cleaned off my face and tried to act sympathetic.

"At least you didn't get your shirt dirty," she said with a smile.

Later that evening, Uncle Joe brought up another big dish of ice cream. I never flicked his newspaper after that.

One more thing about the basement: Uncle Joe, before he became a house builder, was a TV repairman with my cousin Phil. Around 1950, they hand-built a TV and put it on a table in the basement. It had about an eight-inch screen and was built like a tank. This was a very big deal!

We set up chairs in the basement, and, with some of the neighbors, each night we watched the only few hours that TV broadcasted. I remember one program I think called "Lights out!" It opened with this face on a black background and a crashing organ sound. It scared the shit out of me.

All the houses had front porches or stoops—on both the lower and upper floors. Some were enclosed, but most were open. In the humid summer nights before air conditioners, we all sat on the porches to keep cool and socialize with the neighbors. When I was really small, I sat for hours counting and naming the cars that drove by. By the time I was four, I could name every car made—except for the expensive ones that never drove down our street.

On the corner was Barbaro's grocery store. A hard-working bunch, the whole family worked the store—the father, mother, and three kids. It was open seven days a week until 11 PM. You have to be impressed by a 119-hour workweek. Wooden floors and counters, it had the smell of an old country store. We went there for nickel sodas, candy bars, and, once in a while, for bread and milk.

McCarroll's Meat Market got most of our business. It was kind of a mini-supermarket with fifties-modern brick, Formica, and air conditioning. Sometimes, we'd go there just to get out of the heat. My mother sent me there every Thursday for meat for sauce. I still remember the instructions: two pounds of stew beef and a half a pound of pork, ground once. I gave Mrs. McCarroll two dollars, and she gave me change!

Next to McCarroll's was The Garden Grill, the neighborhood bar. In those days, Albany was controlled by a big Democratic machine and run by Dan O'Connell, a crusty old Irishman. The politicians and local contractors hung out in this Irish-type pub. It had a small back room where you could get a pitcher of beer for a buck, also sandwiches, a corn beef dinner, and of course, boiled eggs.

At night, there was a tougher crowd, or maybe it was the same crowd, just drunker. Many times we'd be sitting on our second floor front porch, keeping cool, and a fight would spill into the street. My father would get out his accordion and play the Gillette Razor song while they were fighting—pretty funny. (Gillette sponsored the Friday night fights on TV.)

Mami Bloodheim's candy store was a block down the street. Mami was about 100 years old, stood about 5 feet tall, and was always miserable. She lived in this little cottage, where she converted her living room into a candy store. Yards of penny candy, trinkets, an ice cream freezer, and a soda cooler were crammed into this tiny room. Oh yeah, she sold fireworks in the summer. To this day, I feel guilty about our buy one/steal two policy.

Everything I thought I needed in life was within walking distance.

A block north was the neighborhood park called McGowan's. It was run by the city, and in the summer we played horseshoes; "Unigoal," a basketball game without a backboard; volleyball; and softball with the biggest, softest ball I'd ever seen. It was about 5 inches in diameter and weighed about a pound. It was so heavy that sometimes a person would fall down trying to catch it. Mark McGwire, at his chemically enhanced best, could maybe hit it 100 feet.

At the end of the summer, we stole all the equipment so that we could play in the winter or at least the fall. The city always hired some twit to act as the "park teacher." We disrupted everything these park teachers tried to do. Women were particularly vulnerable and never lasted longer than a summer. Some quit after a week.

One block south was the city dump—sounds bad but it really wasn't. On one side of the dump was The Fred Green Little League Stadium, and on the other side was Krank Park, my Little League home where I had my famous never-win career as a starting pitcher of the 0–18 DeWitt Clinton team. Krank Park was incredible.

The Italian contractors banded together and built the most beautiful stadium imaginable. There were covered bleachers, real dugouts, a concession stand with homemade Italian sausage and peppers, an electric scoreboard, red sand from New Jersey for the infield, and fresh sod every year for the outfield. Graffiti? Only if you had a death wish! It was so amazing that they played the playoffs to the Williamsport Little League World Series there—in spite of the dump.

Each block had a personality. Most people on our block took care of their homes. They were painted regularly. The grass, what little existed, was cut weekly. Ethnically, the block was mixed. There were about 40 percent Italian, 40 percent Irish, and 20 percent other people. No Blacks, Asians, and very few Jews except for Mami Bloodheim, the candy store lady, and Max Rosenberg, who owned the small grocery store about three blocks away on the corner of Slingerlands and Second. A block south was a row of three-story tenement buildings. It was where the "Cooties" lived—more about them later.

My cousins, the Nuciforos, lived next door. Old man Nuci was a boot black. He shined shoes downtown near the capitol building. He must have made some money because he owned the house and raised five kids—four girls and a boy. His son, Joe, was my dad's age and played bass in a band. He moved in upstairs when he got married and had two sons, Dominic and Anthony.

Dominic had a rock and roll band as a teenager. It was called Dominic and the Imperials. They knew about three songs: "Louie, Louie," "Twist and Shout," and "Shout"—all of which sounded the same but with different words. They weren't bad except they had trouble ending a song together. When I was in college, I booked entertainment for fraternity parties. I booked Dominic for the frats that were on a budget. The band got $5 each and $10 for Dominic—about $35 or $40. I would charge the fraternity about a hundred and keep the difference. Whenever Dom asked for a raise, I told him to learn ten songs, end them together, and then we'd talk.

In Nuci's backyard was a cherry tree. No ordinary tree, but a Rainier. I didn't know what that meant until forty years later when I saw them selling at Gelson's market for $7.99 a pound. The tree was amazingly fruitful. It must have been there for fifty years.

I was the official picker, principally because everyone else was either too old or too fat. They'd send me up with a basket and rope. I'd tie the rope around a branch and secure the basket. When the basket was full, I lowered it. They emptied it, and I pulled it back up. My grandfather DePalma would sit in the yard drinking a glass of wine and smoking his "De Napoli" and yelling: "Carlucci, whena you picka the cherries, I wanta you to whistle…I don't heara you whista…ling!" he sang play-fully. It's hard to eat cherries when you're whistling.

2

The Family

Technically, I am a second generation Italian American, but growing up I felt as if I was living in Calabria. Short, fat women dressed in black (in case anyone died they were ready) surrounded me. They proudly wore a gold tooth somewhere in their mouths and knitting needles in their hair. They had boobs the size of Rhode Island, and those medical-looking tied shoes covered their support nylons that were, for reasons unknown, rolled down to their knees. I guess it was a poor person's version of the fashionable ballet ankle warmers. This was the picture I had of all my first-generation aunts and cousins. They spoke at a frequency that was two octaves above middle C and were always demanding to be kissed.

The Ladies Hold Court

"Hey, Carlucci, comma ova here and giva you Aunt Angelina a biga kiss!" It seemed as if I was always running away from those terrorists.

My immediate family was different. I had a sister three years older, a brother nine years younger, and we were all very American.

My father, Frankie, was a musician but worked during the day at the NYS Motor Vehicle Department to make ends meet. A good-looking Sinatra type with thick black hair and a very deep voice, he played accordion with the Joe Cosco trio. Cosco played bass, and Jake Del Giacco played guitar. Musicians were always coming to pick my dad up for a job, and they regularly brought me something like an ice cream or a candy bar. I loved those guys. They had names like Bassadi, Ippolito, Bandini, Corzini, and Costello. All the names ended in a vowel. They played weddings, Bar Mitzvahs, and club dates. Club dates were one-nighters at clubs in the Catskills, Adirondacks, or local restaurants. They were pretty hip guys and were always teasing and telling jokes. They also did some serious drinking. It was a miracle they were able to navigate those mountain roads with a belly full of Johnny Walker.

I always knew when my father was drinking. He quietly came into my bedroom after the job about 3 AM. He sat on the edge of bed. It was always two or three of the same topics.

"Son, are you sleeping?"

"Ah, no, Dad," I said, half asleep.

"Son?" he repeated softly.

"Yeah, Dad, what is it?"

"Love your mother."

"What?" I said, knowing what was coming.

"Love your mother."

"Right, thanks, I do, Dad."

"I loved my mother."

"Yeah, I know," I said patiently. "Can we talk about his tomorrow?"

"Blood is thicker than water. There is no one closer to you than your mother. Then come your sister and brother."

"I got it, Dad."

"You won't forget?"

"No, but thanks for reminding me."

"Son?" Starting to get a tear in his eye.

"Yes, Dad."

"Don't be a fool!"

I was now awake. There was a pause.

"Mom!" I shouted, "Get Dad."

My mother never went to sleep until my father got home, no matter how late. She came in my room and lovingly escorted my dad out the door and into bed.

My father was such a great loving person that I never really minded these nocturnal visits. He only drank when he went on these club dates. I am sure it was because they always gave the musicians free drinks or the patrons would buy him drinks. He was always very frugal about spending family money. He probably wouldn't stand up to today's Dr. Phil's standards for being a good father because he was always working. We didn't play baseball or fish together, but he was always there. He was totally unselfish with his money, his heart, and with his ear. In my mind, he was the best.

I remember when a small, pretentious French restaurant called the Petit Paris opened in town. They were looking for a musician to play that single note, left-bank-style of French accordion. My dad was hired and played there for what seemed to be years. It turned out that it was about six months. Their big claim was their "flaming sword filet mignon." They cooked your steak, put it on a sword, sprayed it with booze, lit it, and paraded it to your table. As a treat, my mother, sister, and I went one night for a dinner on the house. I didn't even know what a filet mignon was, but we saw my father in action.

I'm not sure how well my dad liked the little Frenchman who owned the place. Dad wrote a song that he sang whenever a steak was delivered. I still remember his sense of humor.

It was sung to the tune of "The Sheik of Arabic."

> *I am the chef at the Petit Paree'*
> *I love to cook you see.*
> *I prepare the flaming sword.*
> *Your check is my reward.*

The Frenchman liked it. I don't think most people heard all the words. The last line was a perfect example of his sense of humor.

My dad had endless stories about his music escapades. He started playing when he was seventeen in the "speakeasies" and "gin mills" in downtown Albany. He claims that just before he married my mother, Tex Ritter, the singing movie cowboy, asked him to tour the country.

"I loved your mother so much that I stayed and married her instead," he said proudly.

"If I had gone," he went on with the twinkle in his eye, "your mother would have married someone else, and you wouldn't be so good looking. See how lucky you are?"

Dad and the Band

His best stories were about Jake, the guitar player. Jake apparently never learned to read very well, which was surprising, because his brother was a doctor. One night Joe, Jake, and Dad were driving on the country road in the Catskills looking for a hotel. They were lost. Suddenly, they came upon a deer crossing sign.

Jake turned and announced, "We must be close to the hotel."

"Why do you say that, Jake?" my dad asked.

"Because we just passed a sign that said, Caution, Dancers Crossing."

My dad looked at Joe and smiled.

On the way home that night, the left rear tire went flat. They got out of the car to evaluate the problem.

"Too bad there aren't any streetlights on this road. It's going to be hard to fix the tire in the dark," my dad said discouragingly.

"No problem," Jake said. "Let's just turn the car around and put the headlights on the tire."

My mother was baptized Yolanda, but somewhere along the way became Viola. She was raised in a little village about fifteen miles north of Albany called Waterford. My grandfather worked on the Barge canal in that area and then became a watchman at the local shirt factory. There were five children: four girls—Viola, Emma, Ida, and Lena—and a boy, Armando. They lived on the top floor of a tiny house where the girls shared the same bed. He rented the lower flat to help with the house payment. My grandfather, Francisco DePalma, raised this family on about $20 per week. Remarkable, isn't it? They all were fed, clothed, schooled, and he owned the house.

In spite of this poverty, my mother possessed a natural elegance. She carried herself with grace and dignity. People used to say she looked like the Queen of England. To this day, at eighty-eight, she is as graceful and beautiful as ever.

She maintained a simple, humble demeanor. I remember she told me how excited she was when she got married and she got a refrigerator. It was a big deal for her.

With only an eighth-grade education, she was remarkably wise. She was a great housekeeper, and we always had clean clothing and lots of food. The joke was that if you dropped your shirt she'd have it washed, pressed, and hanging in the closet before it hit the floor—not far from the truth.

Queen Mother and Baby Coose

She watched the money like a hawk and was able, with very limited funds, to eventually acquire two homes, educate three children, and be independent after retirement. She ought to teach wealth management at the Harvard Business School.

Although the immediate family was small, the extended family was enormous. The families migrated from the southern part of Italy between 1905 and 1920. My grandfather had three brothers, and my grandmother had four sisters and a brother.

My mother had four siblings so that when you add it all up with marriages and children, the number became pretty large. There were the Scavellos and Scavullos, the Cusatos, the Torres, De Palmas, Benardos, Curiones, and the Marchios, the Padullas, and the Pazullos. It went on and on. Originally, they all lived within a few blocks of each other and formed the entirety of their social life.

Every Sunday, we all gathered at Grandma Cusato's for dinner. She fed between thirty and forty people. It was a real madhouse. As kids, we ran through the house, jumped on the beds, threw pillows, and slid down the banister. I don't know how the adults put up with us. My favorite thing was cracking walnuts in the door. We opened the door, put the walnut by the hinge, and then slammed the door shut. It was messy but effective.

The circus started about noon and would go until seven or eight at night. To this day, I have no idea who paid for it all. There was fruit cocktail, two or three kinds of pastas, a baked ham, chicken, calamari, and scungilli; sometimes a turkey. There was eggplant, scadole (escarole), and desserts like cannoli, rum cake, and melon, or, as my grandmother used to say, "mushamello."

After dinner we played cards. Mostly, we played a game called society crap. Kids and adults played together for pennies. Each person would get ten cards—2, 3, 4, 5, 6, 8, 9, 10, J, Q. The Aces, sevens, and Kings were set aside. The cards were placed in front of each player face up in two rows. Everyone would ante up a nickel. Each person would roll the dice. When the number rolled corresponded with the card, the card was turned over. The player continued to roll until a seven or turned-over number appeared. When that happened, the player put a penny in the pot and the dice moved to the next player. The first player to turn over all ten cards won the pot.

The other card game was called seven and half. I think it was an Italian game. Played much like Baccarat, the 8, 9, 10s were removed. The picture cards counted as one-half. You were dealt one card. You could hit or stay. The closest to seven and half without going over wins the pot. My grandfather DePalma and I would play one-on-one. We both cheated every chance we got.

Mock wedding at the yard picnic

Dad and Nuci

In those days, the families were the social circles. We had big picnics at Thatcher Park—the state park about twenty miles out of town—or we'd meet in someone's backyard. Always plenty of food and drink, they would play cards or dress up and do mock weddings or funerals, or make fun of someone in the family. It was hysterical. I had no idea that I was poor.

Since most everyone had a trade, you could get your pants altered by Uncle Tony, the plumbing done by Sonny, the door fixed by Uncle Joe, your hair cut by Grandpa Cusato. Carmine had the beauty salon and my dad's wedding present was to provide music at your reception. The little stuff was free. The bigger stuff was at a substantial discount. God forbid the regular price was ever charged. All in all, with some minor bumps, the system worked well.

There were minor scandals and petty disruptions but nothing ever really major. There was no concept of psychiatry. People were never crazy. They were just a little funny or had funny ways. Even when someone would get in big trouble, it was rationalized away with "…But he has a big heart," or "He was always good to his mother."

There were, however, from time to time "well-intentioned *mis*understandings." For example, it was considered good luck to have a bag of water dropped on you as you left your wedding reception. Well, at Aunt Rosie's wedding, Uncle Patsy waited at the second floor window with a bag of water, and instead of the bride walking out, his brother Dominic walked out carrying presents. The bag of water hit him in the head, broke his glasses, he fell down the stairs, and sprained his ankle. They didn't talk for a year!

Patsy and Dominic, or "Mustacchi," as we called him, were my grandfather's brothers, but they never really got along. They were very competitive. One day when I was about six, they decided that they were going to take me to the carnival, one of those small traveling shows that would show up every summer for a week. I think it was called the James M. Straight Show, or something like that.

Neither of them drove, so they picked me up and we went by bus. I got on the bus, immediately walked to the back, and sat down. In the meantime, they began arguing about who was going to pay my fare.

They made such a commotion that after a few minutes the bus driver got so angry that he threw them *both* off the bus.

As the bus took off, they realized that I was still on it. What a sight! They were jumping up and down, yelling at each other, pointing, as the bus disappeared down the street. I remember thinking that I'd go to the carnival without them, but then realized that I didn't have any money. I got off the bus at the next stop, and began walking home.

It was only about ten minutes away. As I am walking, the next bus passed me with Patsy and Mustacchi on it. They saw me, and started pointing, yelling, and trying to get off the bus. The driver wouldn't stop until the next bus stop. I just waved and kept walking. When I got home, my mother asked what happened. I told her to ask them.

"They should be back in few minutes," I said nonchalantly.

I changed and went out back to play. I never did get to the carnival that year.

3

The Grandfathers

My two grandfathers were dramatically different personalities. My father's father, Carlo, was a small, delicately featured man who worked as a barber. A serious type, he worked six days a week and didn't take a vacation in forty years. He worked next to the capitol building, and most of his clientele were, or worked with, state legislators. He worked right through the Depression cutting hair, shaving, and massaging the heads of the politicians—not a small feat, considering 25 percent of the country couldn't find work. I think it was his contact with educated men that made him appreciate the value of an education so much.

Carlo, Second Chair at Paladino's

When he got married, he moved into my great-grandmother's house on Jefferson Street in the heart of the Italian district. All the "gumbas" lived within a two-block radius. It was a small brownstone with a cement stoop where everyone would congregate. My great-grandmother and Aunt Rosie lived on the first floor, and my grandfather and grandmother lived on the second floor where they raised two kids. They shared a kitchen, a small backyard, and a basement with a wood-burning stove.

My great-grandmother, Victoria, was old and partially blind when I reached my hyperactive period. I used to run around her house and make Indian noises. She got so nervous that she kept trying to trip or hit me with her cane. I grabbed her cane during one of her swings, and she fell off her chair, landed face first on the floor, and her nose began to bleed. Obviously, nobody was very happy with me after that incident. Fifty years later, I still hear the story about making great-grandmother fall and giving her a nosebleed. She died about a month after the incident.

My grandmother and I were very close. She would always carry gum or candy and bring éclairs or cream puffs when she visited. When I was older, I loved asking her about the old days. She was amazingly candid.

"So where'd you go on your honeymoon, Grandma?" I'd asked.

"Upa-stayza," she said.

"Where's that, in Russia?"

"No, upastays, upastayza," she repeated.

"Oh, upstairs, you honeymooned upstairs."

"Si!"

"Oh, that must have been exciting," I smiled.

"Couldn't make too much noise. The walls were lika paper. Ina the morning, you hanga the sheet on the clothesline," she said with a devilish smile.

"Well, that's more than I needed to know," I said, beginning to blush.

The sheet had something to do with proving to the neighborhood that the bride was a virgin.

She was a strong, hard-working woman with a gigantic heart. When someone needed help, she was the one to go to. I loved her. She was great. She not only controlled the money but also my grandfather.

Carlo was a kind and generous man, but when he wasn't, my grandmother filled in the gaps. I was told that I was special to him because I was the first grandchild, and I had his name. Unfortunately, we never really connected. When I was little and the whole gang was down for Sunday dinner, I would climb onto his shoulders while he was sitting in the lounge chair and make like I was playing the drums on his bald head. I know he hated it. He would yell out to my mother and say, "Viola, would you please control your son?"

He never drank or smoked or gambled. He worried about everything and had difficulty making small talk. I think that was because he was just shy or self-conscious. He *did,* however, cut the hair of everyone in the family, never charged a nickel, and never complained.

Sadly, not too long after he retired, he fell ill. My grandmother, the saint that she was, fed him, bathed him, and carried him from his bed to his wheelchair. Just before he died, he admitted to me how badly he felt that he didn't enjoy life more. He never spent money, so that he could enjoy it when he retired. As it turned out, most of his savings went to the doctors and the hospital. He was delighted, however, to see his first grandchild graduate from college.

My mother's father was truly the antithesis of my father's father. A tall, statuesque man with large, rough hands and big burly chest, he stood over six feet tall with a big head and round face. Francesco DePalma had a relaxed, easygoing quality and was quick-witted in spite of his limited education. His favorite line to me when I acted up was "Carlucci, you'da better behave, or I'ma gonna locka you up in the shendee (the shed) and let the rats eat you!"

Pa DePalma

The Grandfathers, Carlo and Francesco

He served, for a brief time, in the Italian army. When he migrated here in the early part of the century, like many immigrants, he got a job working on the Barge Canal in Waterford, New York. The five high-lift locks built in the Troy/Waterford area are, still today, an example of the finest locks built in the world.

Later in life, he worked as a watchman for Cluett-Peabody, the company that made Arrow shirts. The plant was about a mile from his home. The railroad ran down the middle of his street. He would walk on the tracks over the trestle bridge spanning the Mohawk River to the plant. He walked it four times a day. Each day he came home for a hot lunch, usually a big dish of pasta or "pasta fagiolo." In the evening, after dinner, he relaxed on the back porch in his favorite rocking chair, sipping his homemade "dago red," and puffing on that smelly Di Napoli cigar.

He was retired when I started spending time with him. Each summer, I packed my suitcase and moved in with him for about a month. It was like moving to the country. The house was about two blocks from the river. I still remember waking in the morning to the faint smell of creosote. Creosote was a tar-based preservative that coated trestle bridge wood and the giant wood beams on the docks. The scent had the intoxicating quality of gasoline and was unforgettably strong.

I made friends with the kids in Waterford, and we spent the days riding our bikes, walking the tracks, and swimming in the river—a real Huck Finn experience. I was forbidden from swimming in the river because at that time it was a little polluted. Actually, it was a lot polluted. To this day, my mother never knew what went on. If she did, she would have had heart failure. We not only swam in the river, but we jumped off the trestle bridge. Not only did we jump off the trestle bridge, but we once played chicken with the train. The bridge was about 30 feet above the water and very scary. To be perfectly truthful, I only did it twice: once without the train and once with the train. Of course, we bragged that we did it all the time and that it was 100 feet high, not 30—more macho nonsense. In reality, I was so scared after I jumped with the train coming that I couldn't stop shaking for an hour. I still get a chill thinking about it. Without question, it was one of the dumbest things I have ever done.

Ironically, it was the same day that I was caught swimming. My mother was visiting and the smell of river on me was overpowering. I was grounded for the rest of my stay.

As it turned out, the grounding wasn't so bad, because part of the reason for my being there was to help my grandfather make wine and tomato sauce. Once a year, Grandpa De Palma, or "Pa" as we called him, would make wine and tomato sauce and distribute it to the family. He and I made the wine, and then the following week, all his daughters would help with the sauce.

Sadly, as often as I did wine with him, he never really gave me the recipe. It was called "Dago Red." I recently checked the Internet and found a recipe that looked very close to the one he used:

Dago Red (recipe makes 5 gallons)

70 pounds of any black wine grape
4 tsp pectic enzyme
1/2 to 3/4 tsp potassium metabisulfite
3 tsp yeast nutrient
1 packet red wine yeast

- **Wash and crush grapes, then move them into primary.**

- **Adjust acidity to 6.5 grams per liter and sweeten if necessary to bring specific gravity to 1.088 if necessary.**

- **Sprinkle 1/2 teaspoon potassium metabisulfite on grapes and stir in well. Cover primary and let sit 12 hours.**

- **Sprinkle pectic enzyme on grapes and stir in well.**

- **Recover primary and let sit another 12 hours. Add yeast nutrient, stir well, and add activated yeast.**

- **Cover the primary again and set aside. Punch down the cap daily, stirring juice as you do so.**

- **When vigorous fermentation subsides and specific gravity is below 1.020, press and transfer juice to secondary.**

- **Fit airlock and ferment to dryness. Rack, adding 1/4 teaspoon potassium metabisulfite stirred in well. Top up and refit airlock.**

- **After wine clears, wait 30–45 days and then rack again, top up and refit airlock. Wait additional three months, stabilize, sweeten to taste, wait ten days, and rack into bottles.**

- **Age three months before tasting.**

May require additional aging.

Sounds like something a chemical engineer might make. I can't imagine that Pa knew anything about adjusting acidity and specific gravity. If he did, he called it something else.

He had grapes growing in the yard but he always bought the grapes for the wine.

The grapevines in the yard were pretty cool, though. He built a trellis from the alley around the "shendee" and along the walkway leading to the house. Over the years, the grapes grew over and through the trellises and provided not only delicious grapes, but also shade on a warm summer's day.

They had a wonderful smell. The grapes were sweet. Unlike the kind in the market, they had thick skins. To eat them, you'd squeeze the skins and suck the insides into your mouth. Then you'd suck on the skins until the juices were gone and spit the skin on the ground—or at someone you didn't like.

The shendee, as Pa called it, was a small, barn-like structure that was probably built for a horse and carriage. It had little rooms in the front where he kept his tools and junk and a large room with a loft in the back. It was made of old, unpainted wood and had a hay and mildew smell. Who knew what grew or lived in there? It had little secret compartments to crawl through and hide in. It was an exciting place for an eleven-year-old.

The wine-making started like this. At about seven in the morning, a truck pulled up in the alley. On the truck were pallets loaded with boxes filled with grapes. The driver lowered the pallet to the alley. Pa signed the packing slip. Each box weighed about ten pounds. I carried the boxes, one at a time, to the top of the basement door and stacked them neatly.

Pa would say, "Neat is just asa easy asa no neat."

The basement steps were so steep that it was like walking down a ladder. I later found out why the steps were steep: the dirt floor was crooked, and the inside looked like a mine shaft. Pa had actually dug out the basement by hand. Imagine digging a 20-foot by 20-foot hole 6 feet deep under a house.

I remember telling him what I thought was a clever joke. When I saw that he had to tip his head because the ceiling was so low, I said, "You know, Pa, if you vacuum the floor, the ceiling will get higher."

He didn't think it was funny, either.

The basement was dusty and smelly, mildew mostly, because the basement would flood whenever it rained heavily. At the bottom of the stairs to the right was a hand-powered wine press. There were wooden racks for bottles on the back wall. A half-dozen giant glass jugs lined up to the left. They looked like the oversized bottles that fit into a water cooler. There were bushel baskets filled with empty soda bottles.

I took the grapes from the boxes and washed them down with the hose. I then took a pile of grapes down the stairs and dumped them into the press. After he squeezed the juice out, he poured it into one of the giant jugs. He then added some sugar and some other stuff and corked the jug. When all the jugs were filled, sweetened, and corked, we'd call it a day.

The next morning he went back down to add what I thought was yeast and some other stuff, stir it up, and leave it. Each day he "punched down the cap," which was the crap that grew from fermentation, stirred it up, and corked it again. Magically, one day it became wine.

He always saved some from the previous year. Judging from the condition of the bottles, some of that "dago red" was pretty old. At the end of the day after dinner, he would fill up a Dixie cup with wine and give it to me. I slept like a baby!

It was 7 PM on the following Monday when another truck arrived in the alley. This time it was loaded with bushel baskets filled with locally grown tomatoes. I carried a basket into the yard. It was so heavy that I decided to use an old, rusty kid's wagon that I found in the shendee. It worked great. It held two baskets.

My mother and her sisters appeared with a large metal tub, the kind used for dunking apples. She then turned on the hose and filled it with water. A hand-cranked meat grinder was clamped onto a table that had been set up in the shade of the grapevine trellis. The hand crank had been removed, and replaced by a radiator-looking belt attached to an electric motor. This was Pa's contribution to bringing technology to the tomato sauce process.

After the tomatoes were washed, we cut them cut into quarters and put them into a pot. Two more pots were used: one at the front of the grinder to catch the juices and one at the back to catch the solids.

The motor was turned on and production began. When the juice pot was filled, it was moved to another area for bottling. The pot filled with solids was carried to the garden and dumped into a hole. It was used as fertilizer.

The family collected soda bottles. Along with the empties from the previous year, the bottles were boiled in water and put in baskets waiting to be filled.

With a scoop and a funnel, we filled each bottle by hand. We then placed a piece of fresh parsley and basil in each bottle.

The capping machine looked a little like today's fancy wine openers. The bottle was placed on the stand. The soda cap was placed on the opening of the bottle. The crank swung over top, and the gears pushed the capping rod downward, sealing the cap to the bottle. The production was well organized, and in two days we bottled nearly two hundred fifty bottles.

Pa had cut about an 18-inch section from a metal barrel. He then cut an opening in the front and filled it with wood. It was placed under a metal stand that held a big metal barrel. The barrel was about 5 feet high and 3 feet round. I was lowered into the barrel, and one by one, he handed me the capped bottles of tomato sauce. I layered them down on their side very carefully so as not to break the glass. As I added bottles, I would get taller. Eventually, the barrel was about 80 percent full. I climbed out, grabbed the water hose, and filled the barrel with water. We lit the fire and kept it burning until the water boiled. We let it cool overnight.

The next morning we drained the water through a drainage hole Pa had built at the bottom of the barrel. I then climbed back in and handed the sterilized tomato sauce to my grandfather. Each of his daughters got six bushels of bottles.

He kept all the wine!

4

The Sounds and Smells
of the Street

I have been lucky in that I made friends easily. I had neighborhood friends, grammar school friends, high school friends, college and theater friends, and finally business friends. They were all vastly different and most never met, but I was able to get along with them all.

My neighborhood friends were street kids. They had nicknames that were a variation of their real name, their ethnic background, some physical defect, or some bad behavior for which they were known.

There was Big Dag (short for Dago) and Little Dag. Big Buck Tooth (because his front teeth were parallel to the ground), Cosign, Nickodemous, Clods me Dods, John Dirty Hands, Bugsy, Ignorant Louie, Turk, Judy No Chin, Monk, Lance Boil, Fat Wilfred Whorie Dorie, and Rosie Rotten Crotch. I was Big Coose and my brother, Richard, was Little Coose.

In those days, we didn't have organized activities except for Little League. We just went out. It is amazing to watch how kids can entertain themselves. They'll find a can and kick it. We played mostly street games and, of course, hide and seek. I was an adult before I learned that "Alee-allee-om-com-free," really meant "all come home free."

They were called street games because we played them "in the street." They had names like "Three Feet over Tokyo," "Head On," and "Street Football." Three Feet over Tokyo was simple. The person who stood in the middle of the street was the "it guy." The rest of us stood on the curb. The "it guy" would then yell, "Three Feet over Tokyo," and everyone took three giant steps off the curb and froze. As long as you didn't move you were safe. We would then try to run to the opposite curb before the "it guy" tagged you. When you were tagged, you joined the "it guy." The last one to be tagged won the game.

"Head On" was the next level of stupidity. Like Three Feet, there was "it guy" in the middle of the street. This time he would yell "Head On." Everyone then ran across the street to the other curb. This time, instead of being tagged, the "it guy" tried to tackle you. Again, once you were tackled, you joined the "it guy" in tackling the others. Since we were playing on cement, there were plenty of cuts and scratches. The last one tackled would be the winner—unfortunately, only after being gang-tackled or piled on.

Every street kid played street football. It was played with four to twelve people. Any more and it got too crowded. The curbs were the sidelines, and two designated cars about 100 to 200 feet apart were the end zones. You couldn't rush the passer unless he took a step forward. It was mostly a passing game. There were several popular plays:

• Stop short, go long

• Go ten steps and buttonhook

• Everybody long

• Run straight for the green Buick and freeze

We played with either a real football or a smaller rubber football. The little ball, usually white with black stripes, was great because you could throw it a mile. Interference was called when the ball hit a telephone or electric wire, a car drove through during a play, or someone was hit by car. In spite of the occasional broken window or dented hood, it was great fun.

Hoffman was a real park. It had two big diamonds, a Little League field, a place to play football in the fall, and an ice-staking rink in the winter. It wasn't a real rink. The park workers made dirt piles in a shape of a rectangle about 150 feet long by 50 feet wide. When it got really cold, they would attach a hose to the fire hydrant and fill it with water. It wasn't exactly Rockefeller Center, but it worked. There was a street light nearby so we could skate at night. As our interest in girls grew, this was a place to go.

During the summer, we played baseball every day. We left the house about nine in the morning, returned for a quick lunch, and stayed until dinnertime. Whether we had two or twenty kids, we found a game to play. If there were a few of us, we played pepper. We would stand in a semi-circle. One guy with the bat would bunt; the others would catch and throw it back. The batter would bunt to each fielder in order. When that got boring, we'd hit pop flies to the outfield. When we had more kids, we played a real game.

In the evening, we played in the Little League. I played at Krank, the park on the other side of the dump, because it had a nicer field and was better organized. Fred Green Little League at Hoffman was just getting started and didn't have all of Krank's amenities. You could say it was architecturally challenged because it didn't have the "gumba contractors" to pull it all together.

Every April, there were tryouts. The Little League was broken into two groups—the farm team for the eight- to ten-year-olds (or older kids who threw like a girl) and the majors for the older kids. The farm teams had T-shirts and hats, while the majors had full uniforms.

If you received a call the day after tryouts, you had been drafted by one of the majors. If you were not called, you returned to the second tryouts where they would divide up the herd for the farm clubs. It was painful if you were older than ten and didn't make the majors.

Local companies or service organizations sponsored the teams. This meant buying equipment, providing for uniforms, and once in a while, springing for a hot dog and Coke after a game. There were names like "Ready Mix Cement," "The Sons of Italy," "Anderson Construction," and "Capozzi Electric." I played on the Dewitt Clintons, sponsored by a local hotel.

When I was eight, I could throw the ball as straight and almost as fast as any twelve-year-old. I was a little big for my age but not much. Unfortunately, the majors drafted me as a pitcher for the Dewitts, or the "dumb wits," as we were called.

We were *not* the most talented group in the league. Every year, miraculously, the Sons of Italy would corner all the talent.

Knowing what I know now, I realize that the Dewitts was the only big corporately sponsored team. The sponsor never showed up. Never bought food. Just sent the check. I doubt if anyone, other than the check writer, knew that we existed.

Conversely, the Sons of Italy was a service organization. At every game there were several members cheering on the team. They were always buying food or taking the kids out to eat. The only downside was if you made an error, they would hurt you.

As a pitcher, I did what I was told. I threw most of my pitches over the plate right in the strike zone. The bigger kids would regularly hit the ball, and my teammates would regularly flub the catch. It was like pitching for the Keystone Cops.

After a while, I started getting stomachaches and couldn't pitch. It was a case of stage fright. I couldn't stand being the center of the mess. Krank, with its great uniforms, announcers, and electric scoreboards, was like playing in Yankee Stadium. We went 0–18 that year, and I retired at the age of nine.

Even though I was a good fielder, could catch anything, and could throw the ball to home plate from the outfield without hitting the ground, I turned in my cleats. A failure before I reached the end of life's first decade. My friends, the coaches, even Fred Green, the name on the stadium, couldn't convince me to change my mind. Within a year, they passed a rule that regardless of ability, no one under ten years old could play on the majors without first playing a year with the farm club. I like to think of it as a tribute to my demise.

Junior Eagles

When the fall arrived, our thoughts turned to real football. Two older guys in the neighborhood—"Roy, the Kraut" and "Amos, the Turk"—decided to organize a team. They were big sports fans, and I guess this was a way of getting their kicks by playing coach. They named the team the Junior Eagles. I never understood why, because there weren't any senior eagles unless they were thinking of Philadelphia.

Money was nonexistent, so our uniforms were limited. I had a blue helmet with a white stripe, a set of shoulder pads that didn't fit, and an oversized sweatshirt. Some guys had just the helmet, while others had the pants with kneepads. No one had a complete uniform except for Stew "the Jew" Goldstein. Stewie was an overindulged child, whom we would torment most of the year except for football season. He owned a regulation NFL football.

It was an eight-man team and the plays were simple—run to the left, run to the right, run to the middle, screen pass, and, of course, the cheesiest play of them all, The Statue of Liberty.

We tried to get games with other neighborhoods but there was always a problem. The games never ended. After every play there was some kind of altercation. Someone would get bitten, punched, or a helmet would come off and get bounced off an opponent's head. Our reputation grew, and our opponents began to disappear. Our season eventually consisted of two or three games.

Our big annual game was with the Cooties. It was always played on Thanksgiving so it was called "The Turkey Bowl." The Cooties were the kids who lived in the three-story, tenement-looking buildings with the front doors always opened or missing. Today, we would call them culturally challenged; then, they were just degenerates. When we would have our annual election night bonfire, their front steps and/or doors were the first to be involuntarily donated.

If we looked bad, they looked worse. They had these aviation-looking leather hats with earflaps, which they would stuff with sponges or paper and use as helmets. In fact, they stuffed paper and other crap all over for protection. They had these ugly wool sweaters that looked as if they just came out of the trash.

We weren't ready for a team portrait, but they looked like they belonged in National Geographic. I have to give them credit, though—they showed up every year with a kind of odd dignity.

This game was the nastiest of them all. We didn't have officials. They were more like club bouncers. I played tailback and earned the name "Cusavage," because when I ran with the ball I would scream. This wasn't some sophisticated strategy, but because the Cooties were so big and ugly. I was scared to death. It obviously worked because I would regularly gain 5 to 10 yards.

The game usually lasted around thirty minutes before all hell broke loose. I'm not sure how it started. Someone was hit, bitten, or told their mother was a whore. Mother insults were very big in those days. Not only punches but also helmets and shoes were flying. It was a real brawl. After about ten minutes, the refs separated everyone.

The coaches' big thing at the time, regardless of the problem, was to line up after the game and shake hands. After about two shakes, another fight started. Sportsmanship didn't really seem appropriate for this event.

Finally, we all went home, happy. One of the reasons was because we had stories to tell for the next year. The lies would get bigger as the years passed to where I overheard someone claim that two people were killed during the game.

It was one of the annual rituals of the neighborhood.

Coose at 13, Dad and brother Rick

5

The Casino

When we weren't being athletic, we were playing cards. On the south edge of McGowan's Park, there was a large, overgrown field that led to a dirt road. It was a few acres of real heavy weeded growth. There was poison ivy, sumac, and that weed that we called "stickers." I hated stickers. When you brushed by them, they stuck to your clothing, especially if you were wearing wool. They itched and were hard to remove completely.

We decided to build a secret casino. We cleared about a 30-foot crawl path about 4 feet high and wide starting at the edge of the park. At the end of the path, where the ground was flat, we cleared about a 12-foot-square area and put down a piece of linoleum that we found falling off the back of a truck that was parked in the A&P supermarket's lot. The entrance was covered by a trap door that we rigged out of sticks and brush. It was really hard to find.

This was true penny-ante gambling. We played for pennies, nickels, and sometimes dimes. We played five- and seven-card stud, three-card draw, jacks or better, deuces and threes wild, baseball with 3s and 9s wild with an extra card for a four and, of course, blackjack. We made up games with so many things wild it was hard sometimes to figure out who won.

The games were generally honest, but we would flip the deck or deal off the bottom occasionally for fun or when things were right. Things were always right when Fat Wilfred played. Fat Wilfred was an overweight, spoiled kid who wanted to be part of the gang. He had an older brother who worked for the electric company. He was electrocuted a week after he started climbing poles—very sad.

Wilfred heard about the casino and begged to play. This is what is referred to as a perfect storm. Wilfred always had money, and we held all the cards. We blindfolded Wilfred and led him down the path to the casino. When we removed the blindfold, he had no idea where he was. All he could say was, "Is this cool? Is this cool?"

We took about five dollars that day from him. It's pretty hard to win when the whole game is cheating. We arranged for others to lose so he wouldn't think anything was wrong. Five dollars was big money. It could provide enough soda and candy to throw the entire gang into a diabetic stupor.

We were very careful. We gave Wilfred a free soda and a candy bar. Just to be nice. It was like a Vegas freebee.

"You got to give some to get some," Louie used to say.

One day, someone decided that it might be smart to let Wilfred win, not a lot but a little. What a big mistake! Wilfred was pulling straight flushes, straights, and four-of-a-kind cards out of his ass. "Clods me dods," who was a little psycho to begin with, started getting crazy. Wilfred was winning too much!

Every time Wilfred won, Clods' head started bobbing and his eyes would dart all over the place. It was really hot that day and we all, including Wilfred, had taken off our shirts. Most of us tied our shirts around our necks to absorb the sweat, but Wilfred threw his in the corner. Wilfred was so fat that he had tits. Clods would reach over and pinch his nipples and say, "Look at the tities, look at the tities." Wilfred hated it.

Everybody was smoking cigarettes and drinking Cokes. Wilfred won another pot. Clods got so mad that he flipped his butt into Wilfred's shirt. Nothing happened!

We dealt again and forgot about it. Suddenly, the shirt burst into flames. There must have been matches in the pocket. Startled, we tried to put it out. Dirty Hands beat it with a stick, but it only made matters worse. Sparks flew and the dry weeds started smoking. We all started yelling and pushing our way up the path. By the time we got to the park, the smoke was billowing into the sky.

Luckily, the firehouse was located two blocks away at the corner of Second and Sand. Within minutes, the siren broke our concentration on the smoke.

Clods looked at the group and said, "Remember, nobody knows nothing! That means you, Wilfred. You say a word and I'll kill ya personally."

"What should I tell my mother happened to my shirt?" Wilfred asked.

"You tell her to stop buying you cheap fuckin' shirts. I saved your life. If you were wearing that rag you'd be dead by now," Clods smiled, obviously pleased with his convoluted logic.

We ran to the other end of McGowan's where Mrs. Lyngarden sold soda and candy out of the back porch of her house. We debated on whether to stay or leave. We decided to stay. If we left, we thought, we'd look guiltier.

By now, the fields were ablaze. A hook and ladder and pumper had arrived and were watering down the fire. We bought some Cokes. They were seven cents including a two-cent deposit for the bottle.

Although our hearts were beating like jackhammers, we tried to look cool and removed as we walked casually back toward the fire. We sat on the grass, mourning the loss of our famous casino. It was a sad day.

One of the firemen, I think it was Frankie Magano's father, walked over to us.

"What do you guys know about this?" he asked.

"About what, Mr. Magano?" We always answered a question with a question whenever we needed time to think or we were guilty.

He smiled knowingly and shook his head, "Someone could have been hurt. You should be more careful next time."

He reached into his pocket and threw some burnt playing cards on the ground. He stared at us for a moment, turned, and walked away. I guess he figured that it was an accident. It was a sad day for us. We couldn't rebuild. The field was burnt to a crisp.

6

The Dump Wars: Part 1

About a mile east of Second Avenue, just north of Krank Park and south of Hoffman, was the city dump. Nobody really thinks about the importance of dumps. We put our garbage in bags, carry the bags out to the trash cans, and once or twice a week a truck comes by and carries the trash away. Out of sight, out of mind.

All this garbage that is collected has to go somewhere. New York is lucky. It puts its garbage on a barge and dumps it in the ocean. Most cities don't have that option and try to locate an area that needs fill. They unload the garbage, pat it down, pour dirt over the top, plant some grass, and voila! A park.

On route to becoming a park, however, a dump is a pretty nasty place. It is the essence of dirty. It is the breeding place for all kinds of disease; it smells awful and is the home of rats and other unsavory small animals.

To the average home-owning adult, it is a nightmare that reduces property values. To eleven- and twelve-year-old kids with a Daisy Red Ryder BB gun, it was a land of adventure.

We all had Red Ryder, lever or pump action rifles. The fancier rifles had sights. We would set up targets in the yard to practice, but our real goal was hunting the dump rats.

A hunting day would begin about nine in the morning before it got too hot. We met at the end of O'Connell Street where old man Nuci had built a two-car garage and tended to a large vegetable garden in the rear. We crawled through a hole in the fence onto an open, overgrown field. There was a footpath about 100 feet long that emptied out by the edge of the "Clay Cliffs."

The Clay Cliffs overlooked the dump. About 150 feet above, the hill dropped at about a 30-degree angle, and then leveled off. The side of the hill consisted of hard white clay littered with trash, empty soda, beer cans, and bottles.

As we left the footpath, we stood at the edge of the cliffs staring out at our next adventure—Nick, Louie, Little Dag, and me. With rifles in hand we looked a little like the Magnificent Seven, minus the magnificent.

To digress for a moment, the Clay Cliffs was a place where we were initiated, showed our bravery, and agreed to perform stupid acts. My act of supreme intelligence consisted of riding my bike down the hill—a feat that had only been successfully done once by "Crazy Richie" Gatto.

The usual gang was there to witness the ritual. "Big Coose" was going to ride the cliffs!

I made it down almost to the end when my front wheel hit a gopher hole. I flew over the handlebars, flipped in the air, and landed on a broken beer bottle. I laid there for a moment to regain my senses. I was more stunned than hurt. As I stood, I noticed a big piece of glass sticking out of the side of my middle finger. Without thinking, I pulled the out the glass. I struck oil. Blood started gushing out my finger. I removed my T-shirt. It was covered with clay. I shook it hard, and turned it inside out. It was the cleanest thing I could find, and I wrapped it tight around my finger and hand. My Cub Scout first aid badge had paid off.

With cheers coming from the top of the hill, Nick grabbed my bike and we headed home.

As I got to my street, I could see my mother standing on the porch talking to my Cousin Phil.

By now, my T-shirt had turned completely red. My face, shoulders, and knees were all scratched and dirty. I walked to the house, and I looked up at my mother who had turned paste white. With her hands resting on her cheeks, all she could say was, "Oh my God, oh my God."

"What the hell happened to you?" Cousin Phil, who was a vet that landed at Normandy, asked calmly.

"I fell off my bike and cut my hand," I said, looking for sympathy.

My mother rushed me into the bathroom, removed the T-shirt, and put my hand into the sink. My hand, covered with blood, made the wound look worse than it was. She washed my hand in cold water and poured hydrogen peroxide over it. It started to sting and fizz up like an Alka Seltzer. I was still bleeding heavily. She took some cotton, stuffed it into the cut, wrapped my hand in a large washcloth, and wrapped it again with an ace bandage.

We walked back outside. Phil, knowing my mother didn't drive, was waiting with the engine running in his '55 DeSoto, ready to take us to the doctor.

Dr. Del Giacco was the brother of Jake, the bass player in my father's band. His office was less than a mile away at the corner of Delaware and Whitehall Road. The nurse brought us right in to the holding room. Within a minute, the doctor opened the door.

He looked at me and said, "Wow, what a mess." He looked at my mother, sensed her nervousness, and said, "Now Viola, don't worry! He'll be just fine. I haven't lost a patient since Tuesday."

It took a tetanus shot, sixteen stitches, a little pain, and I was fixed. He bandaged my hand with my middle finger extended. It was like I was giving the world the perpetual bird.

I looked at my hand and thought, "This could be useful."

The next week at school Sister Dolorata was yelling at me for some insignificant transgression. I sat there angelically with my bandaged hand resting on my heart. Every kid in the class got it and cracked up, except for Sister D. She was too busy listening to herself talk. It was wonderful.

Returning to our day of hunting. There we stood at the top of the cliffs scouting the landscape. We each grabbed a piece of cardboard, shouldered our rifles, and slid down the steepest part of the hill. We walked flanked in a straight line toward the edge of the dump, our cocked rifles in hand, waiting for the action to begin.

The dump is an active place. Garbage trucks arrive and drop their loads. Tractors are pushing the piles around so as to evenly distribute the loads while compressing the garbage. Because this pressure can cause spontaneous combustion, a number of fire hoses are spaced around the work area to keep things wet and to prevent fires.

In addition to the dump workers are the dump pickers. The dump workers are normal municipal workers who are constructively managing the disposition of the city's trash. The pickers are crazy people who live in orange crate shacks in the dump and scrounge around the trash to find whatever they can to buy mostly booze or drugs. They are a mysterious group, because no one knows where they are from or where they are going. It is truly America's underclass. Since our few attempts to be friendly failed, we formally classified them as the enemy.

As we crossed the first edge of the garbage line, we froze and waited patiently. Suddenly, there was a rustling noise. In a flash, the brown spot crossed in front of us. The three of us missed, one of us hit him in the back. It stunned him but he took off down a hole before we could get our second shot off.

Shooting rats with a BB gun takes real skill. If you don't hit them in the head or neck, they won't go down. Some days we spent hours shooting only to come up empty. When we were older, air rifles and 22s made it much easier. Hit them anywhere and they'd go down.

We took another step. This time, a half-dozen of the vermin begin scampering around. Pow! I hit one perfectly. He flipped over on his side. Little Dag stepped up and finished him off. This was a bonanza day. They were all over the place. We were loading and shooting. It was great fun.

We were so focused on the shoot that no one noticed that we had drifted near "Beulah Blue Face's" shack. Beulah was one of the leaders of the pickers and the meanest of them all.

His name comes from a blue birthmark that completely covered the side of his face. His ratty hair and lack of teeth gave him the look of a witch. Nick came up with the name "Beulah Blue Face."

Beulah's shack consisted of orange crates, pieces of wood, and linoleum that he gathered from the dump and tied together with rope and string. There was an old chair and couch. He had an old potbelly stove he used to keep warm at night. He kept it hidden from the dump workers or they would have taken it. Remember, the dump was a fire ready to happen.

Totally by accident, one of our shots ricocheted off a rock and hit Blue Face in the neck. Beulah looked like a pile of rags sleeping on the ground, and so we didn't know he was there. He screamed and jumped to his feet. Little Dag was only a few feet away. With his rags and arms raised, he looked like fuckin' Dracula. It startled Little Dag so badly that he tripped, fell, and dropped his Red Ryder. Blue Face dove at Dag and grabbed his foot. Dag was screaming and squirming. To protect Dag, we started peppering Blue Face with BBs. Dag finally broke free. Blue Face was cursing and yelling all kinds of profanities.

The good news was that Little Dag was free. The bad news: Beulah got his Red Ryder.

The Dump Wars had begun!

The news of the Blue Face incident spread quickly throughout the neighborhood and, of course, the story became exaggerated.

> *The four of us had taken on the pickers in hand-to-hand combat. Louie had cut off Beulah's hand with the machete knife his father brought back from the war. The pickers were prowling the neighborhood seeking revenge by stealing young children.*

It was all bullshit. The entire incident was an accident that lasted about thirty seconds.

The problem with these exaggerated stories is that, after a while, they morphed into the truth.

We made a few attempts to sneak back down to the shack to get the rifle, but Beulah was either not there or he had hidden the rifle. It was fall, and it was getting too cold to pursue it further. We decided to wait until spring before we launched another attack.

7

Girls, Girls, Girls

I was twelve and full of puberty. I went steady that winter with *National Geographic* and a copy of *Playboy*. City kids get the concept of sex instantly. Biologically, the hormones were out of control. Suddenly, there were girls. We noticed them walking down the street, in school, at the ice cream store. They were everywhere. Their fannies were more round, and they were growing boobs. How come I never noticed before?

It was a new kind of excitement. Now skating at night made sense. The girls started inviting us to their birthday parties. There were actually necking parties. We played post office, spin the bottle or just grabbed someone, turned off the lights, and start necking. It was all very innocent and natural—except for Dorothy and her sister, Rosie. They were tenement girls, the feminine version of the Cooties. Without going into embarrassing detail, I had a nano-second affair with Rosie in "Barry O's" basement. It lasted less than a minute and cost me a dollar.

We went from virgins to Don Juans literally overnight. We had broken the ice. What more was there to know? Before it was just groping and petting. This was the big time. This was pussy. Call the newspaper!

The conversation before this monumental event generally went like this:

"Did you get any tit?"

"Yes!"

"Over the sweater or under?"

"Under!"

"Over the bra or under?"

"Under."

"Was the bra unhooked?"

"Yes!"

"Did you see an actual nipple?"

"Yes!"

"Cool!"

Now that we had done the deed, we no longer discussed details. The new conversation was:

"Did you fuck her?"

"What do *you* think?"

"Cool!"

We were feeling very cocky and pretty obnoxious. We heard about the whorehouses on Green Street from the older guys. They were the two-story brownstones with the canopy over the windows. It cost between $5 and $50.

My thirteenth birthday was in March, and it seemed like a perfect time to go big time.

It was about 7 PM on a Saturday night. I told my mother we were going over to Louie's basement to play cards. I grabbed $20 from my paper route money. We picked up the Second Avenue bus across the street from my house. It drove south to Pearl Street and then from Pearl to State. We got off the bus at State and walked two blocks south to Green down by the river.

Green Street was "Sin City." It was mostly populated with blacks. There were a few bars, jazz clubs, a barbecue restaurant, and houses of horizontal refreshment. We never had a problem with the black kids. We played basketball with them at the Boys Club. They didn't bother us and we didn't bother them.

We swaggered down the street and about two blocks down, there they were: three or four houses with canopies on every window. We started to get the giggles. We'd never have admitted it, but we were still kids. We walked up to the door and rang the bell. The door opened and a tall, very attractive black girl appeared wearing a loosely hanging paisley sundress.

"And what can I do for you boys?" she said in a Jamaican accent.

"We're here for a little...little, ah, fun," I replied, trying to hide my nervousness.

"Got any money?" she said in a nice, but patronizing way.

"We each have about five...maybe more," I didn't want to give away the store.

"Five," she started laughing.

Then in a motherly way, she smiled and said, "Okay, come on in."

We walked in past the living room where three or four women sat scantily dressed and sat down at the kitchen table.

"Do you need any help, Sheila?" one of the girls asked.

"No, I can take care of them," she replied.

"Would anyone like some chocolate chip cookies?" she asked in a sweet way.

We paused for second as if we forgot where we were. Louie was shaking his head and about to say yes, when I interrupted, "Ah, no...no, thank you."

I looked at Louie as if to say, *what are you fuckin' nuts? Where do you think we are...at a Girl Scout jamboree?*

"Who's first?" She smiled at me.

"I'll go first," I stood up and walked into the bedroom.

The dimly lit bedroom was furnished with a double bed and two end tables. On one of the tables was a washcloth, a pitcher filled with water, and a bowl. A rocking chair sat by the window.

She dropped her sundress to the floor. Her honey-bronzed body was spectacular. It was athletically lean and shapely.

This is what a real one looks like, I thought. I could hear my heart beating.

"So, your name is Sheila," I said, trying to make small talk.

"Yeah, come here and let me wash you," she said very business-like.

I walked over to the table. She unbuckled my pants, and they dropped to the floor. She then pulled down my shorts and gently began washing my Johnson in the warm water. I took a few deep breaths. I was worried I wouldn't make it past the washing. She patted me dry.

Yes, I...made it! I thought.

She slipped into bed and I slipped in next to her. I suddenly realized that I had no idea what to do next. I awkwardly touched her breast and leaned over to kiss her on the lips. She gave me her cheek. *Stupid,* I said to myself, *you don't kiss prostitutes.*

"Okay," she said, "put it in." I moved over on top of her and we made intense, passionate love for maybe ten to fifteen...seconds.

It can't be over, I said to myself. *Ten seconds!*

I sat up and looked her straight in the eye, "How would you like to make an easy ten bucks?"

She smiled and rolled her eyes. "What do I have to do?"

"Just stay here for another five minutes and make some noise," I answered.

"You mean for your friends...okay." She got it immediately.

I sat next to her while she put on great show. She was moaning and groaning. Ironically, I was learning how it was supposed to sound. I was moving my arms like a conductor, and she was laughing. I think I kind of bonded with her.

After a few minutes, I got dressed and walked back into the kitchen. The guys just stared in admiration.

"Who's next?" I felt like the stud of studs.

In about ten minutes, everybody finished and we started toward the door. Just then the bell rang. Through a crack in the kitchen door, I saw two cops walk in.

"Holy shit, cops!" I whisper-yelled. We ran into the pantry, turned off the lights, and hid in the corner.

"They're gonna arrest us. This shit is illegal. Is my mother gonna be pissed."

Almost five minutes passed. It felt like five hours. Suddenly, the darkness was cut as the door opened.

"Are you sure you guys don't want any chocolate chips?" It was Sheila.

As we walked back toward the bus stop, I looked at my watch. It was 8:30. This entire adventure had happened in less than two hours.

Years of stories, I thought—*years of stories.*

8

Transition

The spring of '57 was a time of change. Everything seemed to be out of whack. Puberty was a time when you had one foot in the nursery and the other in the bar. Look in the mirror and everything is growing out of sequence. The nose is too big. The head is too small. The hair is growing in new places. Coordination is screwed up . The voice cracks. Erections occur regularly for the strangest reasons. It's all very distracting.

Over the winter, our interest in girls increased tenfold, and the related experiences changed priorities.

There were other major changes. Fighting suddenly became important. It wasn't fighting per se, but who was the toughest. It was almost as if the testosterone was demanding a ranking. We sat on the corner discussing the theoretical. Can Louie take Dirty Hands? If the Monk is crazy, and if you made him mad, could he take anyone? A few neighborhood fights grew out of the need for ranking, but not many. We all knew who were the real "dukers."

They were John Dirty Hands, Tommy the Monk P, Clod Me Dods, and Ignorant Louie. They were all "no mercy street fighters," and they proved it repeatedly with fights outside the neighborhood.

My father used to say, "Never fight someone ugly. Never fight someone stupid. And definitely never fight someone who is ugly and stupid." Looking around, I'd say that's good advice.

If you weren't a duker, you had to at least be a "mouth" to achieve any status or respect. I wasn't a duker, but definitely was the number one mouth. Mouths knew things. They were book and street smart, and were good at "sounding" or the "dozens."

These were insult games aimed a person's family, more specifically mothers, sisters, or aimed at some personal defect. The difference between the two was that the "dozens" consisted of rhyming couplets, while "sounding" was just insults. Some examples:

Dozens:

"If you're gonna' to play the dozens you'd better play it fast, 'cause I got your old lady waiting in the grass."

"If you're gonna' to play the dozens you'd better play it cool, 'cause I just balled your old lady in the swimming pool."

Sounds:

"You got a sister, I got her, too!"

"You mama is like a doorknob, everyone gets his turn."

"You mama is like the railroad tracks, she been laid across the country."

"You mama is so stupid, she thinks Peter Pan is a bedside urinal."

These insult games were a way of passing the time when there wasn't much to do, which was most of the time. And most of the time, no one took it personally.

The other major change was that almost everyone was bigger and stronger. I grew about four inches that winter. Dirty Hands, Louie, and The Monk were all shaving. Actually, they had been shaving for a while. They looked thirty, but they were still young teenagers.

It was mid-April and the snow was melting. With the sun, came ambition. We decided that we needed a clubhouse. A private place where we could take girls, have a party, play cards...someplace nice!

Not a hole, or "lean-to" like we built as "kids," but something substantial.

The first thing we needed was to find a site. We found a great spot right off Frisbee Avenue near the Clay Cliffs. We could see in all directions—the dump, the park, and street—but because of the heavy growth and trees it was hard to see in. It was perfect.

We cleaned off about a 15- by 15-foot area, removed all the weeds right down to the dirt. We put some tarpaper down to prevent the weeds from growing.

The word spread quickly and everyone wanted to join. In addition to the usual suspects, we added Fat Wilfred (in case we needed someone to buy sodas), Lance Boil (his father was a dispatcher for a cement company), and Stewie the Jew because he had been a loyal Junior Eagle. The core group grew to ten.

Most of the families in the neighborhood were in some way connected with the construction business. There were carpenters, plumbers, electricians, masons, and, of course, union guys, so that we had access to a good selection of tools and even some materials. We had to scrounge the rest of the materials from somewhere or someone.

The next day we had a "bring your own party." Everyone brought something useful. My father had just replaced the back door on our house, so I brought the old door. We had some lumber, a window, roofing, patio blocks, linoleum, nails, and tools. We lacked plywood and framing lumber.

One of the guys mentioned they were building a Greek church at the end of South Dove Street.

"We should find out whether they're willing to loan us some wood," Nick suggested.

That night, right after dark, Louie, Nick, and I went on a reconnaissance mission. Set back at the end of South Dove Street, in an open field, was the church site. Sure enough, construction had begun. There were piles of plywood—2x4s, 2x6s, and 2x8s—all kinds of goodies. Best of all, there was no fence. It was just sitting there waiting to be borrowed.

It seemed too good to be true. Just as our mouths began to water, a car turned onto the construction site. We jumped behind the wood pallet and watched. It was the guard company car. It had a spotlight mounted on the door like a cop car. It slowly drove around the building and supply area, occasionally shining the spotlight on an area of interest. It stayed about three or four minutes and disappeared down the street.

"Well, that could a problem," Nick noted.

"I wonder how often he makes his rounds?" I asked.

"You wanna stay and count?"

"Not really," a long pause. I looked at Nick and Louie.

"Are you thinking what I'm thinking?"

"Wilfred and Stewie?"

"Wilfred and Stewie would be perfect."

The next day we cornered Wilfred and Stewie at Barbaro's grocery store. I told them now that they were part of the club, they needed to carry their load (an appropriate word for these two).

They were eager to help when I explained the mission.

"Go to the Greek Church on South Dove Street at about 8 PM, stay there until eleven," I slowly explained. "Write down how many times the guard checks the property and the exact time. Do that for the next three nights and don't…don't get caught!"

Off they went. "We'll see on Saturday how well they did."

Saturday morning, I caught up with the two of them as planned at Barbaro's. Their paperwork was outstanding. They had the license, model, and year of the car and the dates and times it drove through. How long it stayed. I couldn't ask for anything more.

I walked outside where the group was sitting on the stoop next to the store.

"The guard comes by every thirty to forty-five minutes," I said.

"Does anybody know how fuckin' heavy a 4x8 sheet of plywood is? How do we carry it the ten blocks to the club site?" Louie complained.

"We need a truck."

"A truck? Nobody's old enough to drive a car," Little Dag broke in.

"My brother has a pickup," John Dirty Hands said.

I forgot that John had just turned fifteen—a year short of a driver's permit, but close enough.

"Hey, John, will he let you borrow it?"

"No, but he works the graveyard shift at the Shell station. He sleeps from six to eleven. And he leaves his keys on the kitchen counter. I've been taking it for little toots for over a year."

The next night we pushed the pickup out of the driveway so as not to make any noise. John neglected to mention that the truck was ten years old and sounded like a fucking washing machine. We drove it down to the construction site. It barely made it. The other guys rode down on their bikes. John's driving was a little jerky. It was a stick, and changing gears was a bit of a challenge.

We parked in front of the last house on the street about fifty yards from the entrance of the site. It was dark, almost 8:30. We turned off the lights and waited. The other guys hid their bikes in the bushes. The headlights of the guard's car appeared and entered the site. He did his usual inspection and drove off.

As his lights disappeared, we went into action. With lights off, we pulled the truck up to the lumber pile and started loading plywood,

2x4s, a few 2x6s, a real bonanza—just what we needed, not one board-foot more. We were not greedy people.

We started down the street still with the light outs, when a pair of headlights appeared at the corner.

"Pull over just to be safe," I said, yanking on John's arm.

Just in time, we slid down on the seat. It was a cop car. The guys on the bikes rode down the street and said hello to the policeman. It was just enough to distract him. The cop rode by and didn't notice the pickup with the lumber hanging off the back. As he disappeared around the corner, we started the truck and, using all the back streets, drove to the club.

We dumped the lumber, covered it with brush, and drove the truck back to John's.

John's brother was still sleeping. We all met down at Barbaro's and celebrated the success of the great Greek church caper!

The great irony, and I would never justify violating one of the Ten Commandments, was that almost a month to the day there was an alleged gas leak at the church construction site, and the place burned to a crisp. It was either a terrible shot of bad luck or someone was building a bigger club. Unfortunately, we never had the opportunity to return what we borrowed.

9

The Clubhouse and the Dump
Wars: Part 2

As we built the club, I realized that there were all kinds of intelligence. The neighborhood guys, while academically challenged, were mechanically precocious. They could measure and cut the wood, hammer, and most notably, plan like journeymen. It was a delight to watch such talent at a young age.

We were building a masterpiece. Lance got his father to give us cement, and we mixed and poured a floor. The framing was square and plumb. It was like a small house. They designed and built a catbird room on the roof. It was about 5x5 with a fireman type pole to slide down. (It was a little more work to shimmy back up.) The catbird room was a lookout to prevent unwanted guests from surprising us—like the pickers.

John Dirty Hands, Louie, and Clods did most of the building. Inside was one big room with a pole in the corner that led to the catbird room. We collected scraps of carpet and eventually were able to cover the entire floor. The inside walls were a collage of pieces of paneling and sheet rock. As we found or borrowed a piece of something, we'd add it. Eventually, most of the inside walls were covered, and what was not we'd patched with fabric.

The building had a door, an old window, and a trap in the back that looked like a big doggie door. We put that in just in case we had to get out fast. We painted the outside a dark green so it blended with the brush and trees.

We had a couch, an old lounge chair, and a table with chairs and stools for our poker games. There was a makeshift potbelly with a tin stovepipe that stuck out the sidewall. It worked great and kept the room warm at night.

Our biggest challenge was light. We tried to steal power from the dump or the street, but nothing really worked. We settled for the light from the stove and candles.

We finished it Fourth of July weekend. We had a great party: hot hogs, hamburgers, some beer, soda, and a bunch of girls. It was as if we had built the Taj Mahal.

It is hard to express how proud we were of our club. One Saturday afternoon, we even invited our families in to see it.

Building the club so distracted us that we totally forgot about the problem that we had with the pickers. One Saturday afternoon, we were just hanging out when Little Dag said, "Let's get my Red Ryder back."

We all agreed that it was time that we paid Beulah a visit. We weren't even sure he was still there. The pickers had a shorter career than an NFL running back. They either went to some shelter or they died. They had to abandon the dump for the winter or they'd freeze to death. It was July, so they were sure to be either re-settled or not there.

We decided to take the diplomatic approach and talk to them. We slid down the hill and walked right up to one of the shacks. About five pickers were sitting there, passing around a bottle of Thunderbird.

"Hey, pickers, where's Blue Face?"

One of the pickers with his back to us turned around. With a look that could kill, Blue Face was staring at us.

"Who are callin' blue face, you little fuckers?"

"Sorry, man, but we didn't know your real name."

Saturated with Thunderbird, Blue Face could hardly stand.

"It's Rufus!" he slurred.

"Rufus?" I said. "What the fuck kind of name is Rufus?" I whispered to the guys.

"It means red for my red hair, you illiterate little prick." He took off his wool cap and sure enough, the reddest hair we had ever seen.

"He looks like a fuckin' American flag: red, dirty white, and blue," I whispered again.

Unfortunately, I whispered a little too loud. "Who you callin a fag? Come over here and I'll take your fuckin' head off."

"Let me slap that old piece of shit," John started his jerky, aggressive moves.

"No, John, you'd probably get infected," I said.

"Look, Rufus, I didn't call you a fag. I said I didn't want to make a real American like you mad. We don't want any trouble. Just give us the rifle back and we're gone."

"You mean the rifle you shot me with."

"It was an accident."

"Anyway I don't have it. They gave me ten bucks for it at the pawn-shop on Delaware."

"Listen, you infected fuck, you get the rifle or we'll come back and kick your asses." John was in rare form.

I looked at the guys. "Okay. Forget it. Let's get outta here for now. The mosquitoes are killing me." The four of us turned and started back up the cliffs.

Suddenly, something stung me in the back of my neck. Another sting hit my hand. We turned. The pickers were lined up holding rocks, a pole, and a long knife. One of them was shooting me with "Little Dag's" rifle.

"You son of a bitch," I yelled, and we started toward them.

Just then we heard a loud boom!

Blue Face was holding a 10-gauge shotgun and had just shot it in the air. We stopped dead in our tracks. *Old Blue Face had certainly sobered up fast,* I thought.

"Next time I see any of you guys down here, expect an ass full of buck shot." His face was full of rage.

We turned and ran up the hill. We could hear them laughing in the background. We returned to the club and told the rest of the guys the story. After we got all the cursing out of our system, we spent the next few hours trying to plan some dramatic act of revenge.

The next Saturday, just before nightfall, we assembled in the club. We blackened our faces like commandos and brought our wool snow hats that we wore pulled over our ears.

"Are you sure of the schedule?" I asked Wilfred and Stewie.

"We checked it Tuesday, Wednesday, and Friday. They go on exactly at 8:45 and go off at 10:00."

"It is important that nobody sees us. We get in, move and secure and get out, no fuckin' around, no tormenting," I said. "I'm worried about the one on the far side. Who's doing that one?"

"We are. We can run the fastest," Dag and Lance answered together.

"Okay, check your watches." There was a long silence.

"Nobody has a watch!" Everybody started laughing like a bunch of goofs.

"I'm getting one for my Confirmation, next year," Clods pointed out.

"All right, all right, fuck the watches. Now, break up into your five teams of two. Each team knows their location. When you move it, make sure it is secure. Okay, it's dark enough. It's about 8:20. We have twenty-five minutes to get down and back. We'll meet at the Clay Cliffs as soon as you can get there. Let's gooooo!"

We all piled out of the club cheering. We broke up into our teams and took different routes to the dump.

Quietly, we inched our way to our destination. There was no one in the dump but one watchman and the pickers. I got to my station with my teammate, John. We lifted it carefully and pointed it directly at the objective. We made sure it was secure and left.

It was remarkable. Everyone performed flawlessly. In any event, we were all back at the cliffs without being detected. We lined up at the edge of the cliffs in a prone position, leaning on our elbows waiting for the show to begin. We had one pair of binoculars.

"What time is it?"

"It's 8:40. We got five minutes."

The five minutes seemed like an hour. Eight forty-five arrived, and nothing happened.

"Hey, Stewie, I thought you said 8:45, exactly."

"I did, maybe your watch is wrong."

Suddenly, like the fireworks on the Fourth of July, it started. We had moved all the fire hoses and pointed them at the pickers' shacks. The water was so powerful that it just exploded them.

With the binoculars I could see Blue Face jumping up and down and screaming. Then, I saw him look around as if he sensed that we were watching. It was as if he had a sixth sense.

"We'd better get out of here before they see us," I said. We crawled out of sight and returned to the club. We sat in the club celebrating our brilliance, recounting the extraordinary sight. We passed the beer around. In those days, a few cans for the ten of us did the trick.

Then Stewie said, "You know, I feel kind of bad for the pickers. Now they're homeless."

"They were already homeless," Louie pointed out. "They should of never shot at us."

It took a Jew to make a bunch of altar boys feel guilty.

The remainder of the summer was pretty quiet. We had won the dump wars. The club was looking great. We even noticed that the pickers had rebuilt their shacks.

It was Labor Day weekend, the saddest time of the year. Summer had ended and in less than a week school started. On Labor Day, we had a BYO picnic at the club for about twenty people. Everybody commented on how cool the club was.

I got home around 10:00 that evening and went to bed. I still remember that night as if it were yesterday. At about 2 AM, I heard a siren. It was no big deal; sirens were going off all the time. We lived only two blocks from the fire station.

Suddenly, I heard another, then another. I got this empty feeling that something terrible had happened. The sirens sounded as if they stopped next door. I got out of bed and walked to the front of the house. My mother, father, and sister were already up and standing on the front porch.

As I looked across the street directly over the roof of McCarroll's Meat Market, I could see flames billowing high in the air, brightening the night sky.

Oh shit, it's either the Koreman house or…or no, the club, I thought.

"Hey, Dad, can I look?"

"Get dressed, I'll go with you," he said.

As we got closer, I could feel the heat from the fire. My worst fears were realized. It was the club!

Everyone from the neighborhood was there. It was the blaze of blazes: a three-alarm fire. All the guys grouped together. No one would admit it, but there were more than one of us holding back the tears. It was very sad. We all loved that club. It was hard to believe that it was gone.

Frankie Magano's father, the fireman, came over to the group. "Two for two, boys." He was referring to the casino fire. He was really angry.

"There will be no more club building, lean-tos, any structures of any kind. I will fine each and every one of you and your parents. They will not be happy. In fact, this structure was so close to being a house, I could fine you even more for not having a building permit. You're lucky the fire didn't spread and that someone didn't get hurt. Does everyone understand me?"

The parents who were standing next to us during this lecture quickly answered on our behalf.

It was end of club building. We never found out how the fire started; however, I can still see the look on Beulah's face on the night of the fire hoses. We could never prove it, but I was convinced it was him.

I guess we didn't win the Dump Wars after all. *Never fight anyone ugly or dumb,* my father's words echoed though my head. Maybe I should add…*or with less to lose.*

10

Not So Great Eight—The Recital

At that time they didn't have middle schools in the parochial school system. By the time you reached the eighth grade, you were ready for something more adult. The cafeteria was filled with kids from kindergarten up. The rules were aimed at serving everyone, which meant you were being treated like a fourth grader.

I was almost 5-foot-10. If it weren't for my baby face, and the fact that I wasn't a nun, I could have been mistaken for a teacher. I was in an awkward time. I felt like a big goof! To make matters worse, I decided to take piano lessons. I already knew how to play chords and understood the piano. My father had taught me all the short cuts. He thought it would be a good idea to get some formal reading training. Big mistake!

The piano teacher was an old nun named Sister Evangelista. She must have been at least a hundred. She was a curmudgeon before I knew what the word meant: cranky, opinionated, a genuine pain in the ass.

I explained to her what I wanted to learn, which she completed ignored. She wanted to start from the beginning to ensure that my fingering was correct and I eliminated bad habits. My first assignment was to learn that piano classic, "At the Zoo." A song written by an idiot, played by idiots, performed for idiots. The lyrics were:

At the zoo
At the zoo
Little monkey
How you do

And the melody consisted of two adjacent notes:

"C-D-C-C-D-C-C-D-C-D-C-D-C"

I could play it with my eyes closed, behind my back, my hands through my legs. Believing that I was being disrespectful to the composer, the good nun proceeded to whack my knuckles with a ruler. My God, this was the first lesson. I begged my mother to allow me to quit.

My dear mother had this thing about quitters, and she believed the nuns were always right. As the year progressed, my relationship with Sister Evangelista worsened, one stupid song after another. Whenever I made a mistake, she'd whack me with the ruler. I was not a happy guy until one day, as she started to whack me, I grabbed the ruler out of her hand and broke it in two. She claimed I assaulted her. My mother was called to school. It was much ado about nothing.

Sister Dolorata made her usual insulting comments, and it was over. I went back to my lesson, only this time there was no ruler. About halfway into the year, Sister Evangelista announced that her students were going to perform in a recital, to which I immediately responded, "Not me!"

I knew immediately that it would be the humiliation of a lifetime. Since I was the only eighth grader taking lessons, and there were no seventh, sixth, or fifth graders taking lessons, the picture was as clear as glass. I'd be one big goof, sitting among twenty little kids. I felt retarded just thinking about it.

Of course Sister Dolorata, loving me as she did, found another opportunity to prove that she could fuck with me anytime she wanted. She held me after school one afternoon. After she had me place all the chairs on top of the desks, she started the arm bending.

"I understand you are refusing to play in the recital."

"You got that right, Sister."

"You're too good to play for the school?"

"No, I'll be the only eighth grader there, among all second and third graders. I'll look stupid."

"Sometimes God asks us to do things that are good for us when it doesn't appear that way."

"God has nothing to do with this."

"God has something to do with everything."

"Hey, God," looking up. "Is it okay if I don't play in this recital…yes? He said it was okay."

"You have no respect for anything. I should come over there and give you a good slap in the face. You will play in the recital or you won't graduate."

"You can't do that."

I was so mad I started to shake. I grabbed a chair and threw it on the floor.

"I not only can but I will. Now, pick up that chair," her face was as red as a stoplight.

"Yeah," I said, "just try it. I am not playing and that's it."

The house was full of parents on recital day. Bucky, Pete, and Billy were there just to make me feel like shit. My recital song was entitled "Swing Prelude."

They always gave the boys songs with masculine names like "Swing" or "March" or "Fight," while the girls got songs with softer names like "Lover's Waltz" or "Flowers in the Springtime."

The recital was just as I imagined, one big retard and twenty little rug rats. I was the first to play. I played as fast as I could, bowed to the audience, and walked right out the back door.

Now that I have the opportunity, I would like to thank the women in my life for making this humiliation possible. For being such a candy ass and for never protecting me against the fascists of the church, I would like to first thank my mother. Next, I'd like to thank Sister Evangelista, the sadistic nun who should get whacked by the big ruler in the sky, and, finally, Sister Dolorata, who must be working under-cover for the devil.

11

The Church

Religion was oppressive in those days. We were forced to go to Mass every Sunday; as altar boys, we also served Mass during the week, plus confession every Saturday, rain or shine. During Lent, we attended Mass seven days a week.

We had Rosaries, Indulgences, Ejaculations (not the good ones), Stations of the Cross, High Mass, Low Mass, Benediction, no-meat-Friday, the nine First Fridays, Good Friday, Holy Thursday, the Holy Days of Obligation, Confession, Confirmation, and, finally, a pass into heaven as you're dying called, Extreme Unction. How's that for ending on a major chord?

This entire structure was designed to provide comfort, create guilt, and raise money.

Weddings. That is how you made money in the altar boy business. Once in a while, someone would throw a five or a ten at a funeral, but it was very rare. People who are grieving don't think of tipping. Baptisms were good, but weddings were the best, always good for ten, and once I got twenty-five.

To be successful, the wedding party had to be worked. We put on our cassocks and surplices and morphed into little angels. One of us would focus on the best man, the other on the father of the bride.

"Hi, we'll be serving the ceremony today if there's anything you need, just let us know," or, *"We're here to help make today as perfect as possible."*

Father B didn't like our hustling the bridal party so we were very discreet. We were the masters of the wedding tip.

The priests weren't stupid. They knew we made money on weddings so they used it as leverage. If you served Mass or a funeral without complaining or screwing up, they'd throw in a wedding. It was all very contrived. It is no wonder why we all became "Cafeteria Catholics" as adults.

In those days, the Mass was in Latin. They taught Latin and how to serve Mass in the third grade. For the next four years, you had the honor of being a servant of the Church. Always available, never paid, never thanked, it was God's work, and you should be thankful for the blessing.

By the eighth grade, we knew all the ins and outs of Catholicism. It was all repetition. The Mass was the same every day. Occasionally, there would be a High Mass for which they would wear fancier garb, add another priest, a few more prayers, which they'd sing in Gregorian, and finally add a choir. All this added a half hour to an hour to the service.

One of my favorites was Benediction. It meant blessing. While I don't remember why we did it, I do remember I liked the smell. There was an Aladdin type lamp on a chain that opened on the top. We poured in some black powdered gum (it was either frankincense or myrrh), lit it with a match, closed the cover, and walked around the altar waving it back and forth. It was actually pretty cool. I have to admit the Church had a great sense of theater. Nobody knew what was going on, but it looked, smelled, and sounded very mystical.

Lent was another big deal. Forty days of being holy. In the third-grade class, I remember the nun would go around the class asking what we were giving up or giving for Lent. Most would say they were giving up candy, soda, or the movies. The good kids would visit the sick or help the elderly. I said that I was giving up school. Everyone but the nun thought it was funny. She sent me to the first grade for the week, again showing great sensitivity and a proficiency in child psychology.

Lent started on a Wednesday. In order to get forty days, it is important to start on Wednesday if you want to end on a Sunday, Easter Sunday, that is. It opened on Ash Wednesday, the day they put ashes on your forehead. If someone in your house smoked, you could avoid going to church by just reaching in the ashtray and making a mark on your head.

We attended the 7:00 AM Mass every day during Lent. The school was next to the church, so after Mass they marched us to the school auditorium where they gave us hot chocolate. I remember they made it with water to save money. Milk is better. Once a week, they gave us Freihofer's Hot Cross Buns. They were delicious.

At the end of Lent was Holy Week. Holy Week started with Palm Sunday, celebrating Christ's triumphal entrance into Jerusalem. There was a big pile of palm leaves on the altar. The priest blessed them and handed them out to everyone in the church. We would then take them home and put them between the mattresses. It was supposed to be for good luck or for fertility. It was the Church's version of splendor in the grass.

Next came Holy Thursday, celebrating the last supper, add one more Mass. Good Friday, celebrating the crucifixion, no additional Mass but add a three-hour service called the Stations of the Cross, during which the crucifixion was celebrated in excruciating detail. Holy Saturday was a day off.

Easter Sunday celebrated the resurrection. This was the highest of the holy days. Why else would my mother buy me new clothes? It was a long service with a number of songs with the word *Halleluiah*. After church, we walked around showing off the new clothes and then went home for a ham dinner and, of course, the candy delivered the night before by the Easter bunny.

When someone is forced to do something over and over and is never given a reason why, it eventually becomes a problem. The old saw that the idle mind is the devil's workshop would probably apply in this case.

Every Saturday, we were required to go to confession. We arrived about 3:30 in the afternoon and waited for the priest, who generally arrived about four o'clock.

Confession is a sacrament in the Catholic Church where you go into this closet and confess your sins. There are three closets, one with a door and two with a curtain. The closet with the door is in the middle and is where the priest sits. The two outside closets are where the sinners kneel. Between the priest's closet and each sinner's closet is a window with a screen and a sliding wooden panel.

After you enter your closet and the priest opens the panel, you say a little opening prayer asking the priest to bless you and telling him how long it was since your last visit. You then begin telling the priest the sins and number of times you committed them. The priest would then give you a penance, i.e., prayers, to say after you left, followed by absolution, which was forgiveness on behalf of God. It was all very cathartic. Sin, confess, sin and confess, it was a lifetime of forgiving a lack of self-control.

One Saturday, as were sitting in the pew waiting for the priest, we began to question our surroundings. We looked around and noticed the only people in the church were the kids and old ladies.

"Are we the only sinners? Where are the high school and college kids and adults?"

"Forget confession, my father doesn't even go to church," Bucky said.

"And what do old ladies have to confess?' I asked.

"Why don't we find out?" Pete said with a chuckle.

"What do you mean?"

"Who would know? The priest goes in at four and comes out at six. Only way we know he's in there is that the people in the pew move over one seat when someone goes in."

"Yeah, we don't even know if he's a priest. All you see is a shadow, and all you hear is a voice," Bucky added.

"One of us could hear confessions, and no one would ever know."

"What happens if we got caught?" I said.

"We won't. One of us will watch the side door, the other by the altar, and third one outside the confessional. When the priest starts up the steps, we'll signal for you to get out."

"For me to get out? Who said I was going in?"

"Look, Coose, you have the deepest voice. If anyone can sound old, you can. And you have a big head like Father B. You'll throw a good shadow."

"I don't know, sounds dangerous," I said.

"Is Big Coose chicken? Bock, bock, bock, bock!" Pete puts his hands in his armpits and started mimicking a chicken. The others followed suit.

"All right, I'll do it, but you better make sure that you give me enough time to get out."

We slipped out of the pew and took our positions. We told the kids in the pew what we were doing and to let the old ladies in after one or two of them got the pew moving."

When no one was watching, I slipped into the priest's section of the confessional.

The first in was Albert the Idiot, Billy G's younger brother.

"Bless me, Coose, for I have sinned. This is so cool."

"Get out, Albert, before you screw things up," I said.

I slid open the other window. It was one of the old ladies.

"Bless me, Father, for I have sinned. It's been one week since my last confession. I took the Lord's name in vain twice. I yelled at my cat four times. I had one impure thought."

One impure thought, mmm, interesting, I thought.

I leaned back. Sat up as tall as I could, and in my deepest voice:

"...And what was that impure thought about?"

"You, Father."

I coughed a couple of times, "Okay," I said, "are you sorry for your sins?"

"Oh yes, Father."

"For your penance, say ten rosaries, say two hundred Ejaculations, and do the Stations of the Cross six times."

"Oh, thank you, Father."

"Absolutete' mumble, mumble in nomina patre, file suae sante, mumble mumble, go in peace, my dear." I closed the sliding door.

I was about to do another one when Pete banged on the door.

"Quick, get out, he's comin'."

My heart started racing. I grabbed the doorknob. It was stuck! I shook it. Finally, it opened. Just as I stepped out, I saw Father B coming around the corner. I fast-walked to the back of the church so as not to arouse suspicion. I ran out the front door and met up with the guys.

"Well, we're dead. We're dead. He saw me coming out of the box. Why did you take so fuckin' long?" I complained. "You were supposed to tell me when he was coming *up* the steps not *in* the church."

"He walks fast," Pete said.

"Great, just great, what are we going to do now? We'll probably get excommunicated."

"How 'bout going to confession?" Billy G said with smile.

There is momentary silence.

"Billy G is a genius!" I smiled. "It's perfect. If we confess it, the priest can't repeat it. It's the law. Nothing that is said in confession can ever be repeated. If he can't talk about it, he can't accuse us. We can't be punished. We're off the hook."

We smugly walked back into church and took our place in the pew.

After a few minutes, it was my turn to go in. I knelt down. My heart was still pounding as the window slid open.

Speaking very quickly. "Father, Son, Holy Ghost, Amen. Bless me, Father, for I have sinned. It has been one week since my last confession. These are my sins. I swore four times. I lied once. I had impure thoughts twelve times. I heard confession once. I touched myself five times. I disrespected my mother twice."

"Wait," father said, "what was that after impure thoughts?"

"I touched…"

"No," he said, "before the touching."

"I heard confession?" I whispered.

"You heard confession!"

"…And I swore forty times, not four."

"Never mind about that, this is a serious matter. People believed you were a priest. They believed they were forgiven. What possessed you to do that?" There was a moment of reflective silence.

"I think I have a vocation, Father. I wanted to see how it felt to be a priest."

"Oh really, I'm not sure whether you should spend some time at Mater Christi seminary or go to law school."

"Yes, Father, whatever you suggest."

"Okay, are you sorry for your sins?

"Oh yes, Father, I'll never do it again."

"For your penance, say three Our Fathers and three Hail Marys."

He gave me absolution and I left. I literally danced to the altar rail and said my penance.

Outside the church, we celebrated our brilliance. We completely believed that we had beaten the system. He didn't even yell.

"What did you get?" I asked.

"Three Our Fathers and three Hail Marys," Pete said.

"Us, too," the rest confirmed.

I turned to Pete, "I just want you to know that was the dumbest fuckin' thing we've ever done. We are really lucky."

In class on Monday morning we were blessed with a visit from Father B. We stood, made the usual greeting and request for his blessing, sat down, and awaited his words of wisdom.

"I have been looking at the Mass serving schedule for the months of January, February, and March. In order to simplify things, I thought we should give longer-term assignments rather than change weekly. This way the boys can develop a better proficiency in Latin and in presenting the liturgy."

What a bunch of bullshit, I thought.

"For January, Cusato and Connell will serve the 5:30 AM Mass, and Farley and Gorezinsky will serve the 6:30 AM. We'll swap in February. Cusato and Farley will do 6:30, and Connell and Gorezinsky do the 5:30. In March, we'll look at it again."

There couldn't be a worse punishment. Albany was Alaska cold in the mornings in winter. Not to mention, we had to get up in the middle of the night.

"Does anyone have any problem with the schedule?" He looked at us with a knowing smile.

"No, Father," we sang in unison. So much for beating the system!

A typical winter in Albany consists of overcast days, freezing temperatures, and between 60 and 100 inches of snow. I begged my father to drive me to church. As usual, he sided with the priest, and he would have nothing to do with getting up at 4:30 in the morning. My mother, bless her, got up and made me some breakfast.

Getting dressed for this weather was an ordeal. I wore a hat with ear lappers, a sweater, a zipper coat, and leggings, buckle boots, and a scarf to protect my face. I looked like the Pillsbury doughboy.

The church was about a mile away. As I walked, the ice-cold wind slapped my face. I walked backwards or stopped at a tree just to warm up my face for a moment. I was miserable.

It took about twenty minutes to get to the church. By the time we arrived, we were half frozen. The church was warm. We walked into the sacristy, which was a room next to the altar. The sacristy housed the equipment for the Mass—the chalice, wine, cruets, in addition to the vestments. The vestments were holy clothes worn by the priest.

We always arrived before the priest to start the set-up. The unblessed wine was kept in a round container behind the altar. In order to get warm, we would go right to the wine and down a ladle full. We'd get a little lightheaded, but it felt great.

Two days before the end of February, and the end of our punishment, we were caught drinking the wine.

Our punishment was extended through March.

P.S. We still drank the wine. We were just more careful.

12

Moving on Up

The remainder of the eighth grade was uneventful. The few school dances and parties aren't worth mentioning. Deciding on where to go to high school was the biggest deal. My choices were limited to Catholic schools or Catholic schools, of which there were two coed regular high schools and one all-boys' military school, where my sister's boyfriend, Jack, soon to be her husband, had just graduated. It was an all-boys' school run by the Christian Brothers, the French ones who make the brandy. Jack spoke highly of the experience.

Founded in 1859 by the Brothers of Christian Schools, the De La Salle Christian Brothers constitute the largest order of men in the Catholic Church devoted exclusively to education. Their roots date back to seventeenth-century France where their founder, St. John Baptist de La Salle, lived with and ministered to the children of the poor.

My parents thought it would be good for me, and so did the nuns and priests at St. James. It was the most expensive and we didn't have much money. I had some paper route money saved, and we had the option of saving additional money by buying used uniforms.

CBA was truly a transforming experience. I was the only one from the neighborhood or my grade school to make this choice. It meant all new friends and experiences. The demographics were very different. It was at a minimum a middle- to upper-class mix, some of whom were very wealthy.

CBA's beautiful campus consisted of a three-story, Georgian-colonial-style school building; a four-story armory to store the guns and other military gear; and a matching building that housed the Brothers who ran the school. It was located on several acres of well-groomed land next to the Albany Law School and opposite the famous Albany Medical Center complex. It was about two miles from home so that I could walk to it most days.

In July, I received notice of acceptance and notice of when the used uniforms would go on sale. As brave and secure as I believed I was, I still had butterflies. I was leaving the safety of the neighborhood for a new groundbreaking adventure.

Three uniforms were required:

The Greens consisted of olive-colored wool pants and a jacket. The jacket was the typical army style with four lapeled pockets and epaulettes on the shoulders. There was a khaki fitted cotton shirt and an olive tie.

For public events, we wore dress blues. *The Dress Blue* was a West Point-looking coat cut at the waist with tails in the back and with a stand-up collar and fifty-two brass buttons. The officers also wore a sword, sash, tar bucket (a hat the looked like a bucket), and a plume.

The pants were matching navy blue with a maroon stripe down the side of the leg. On special occasions, we wore white pants with the dress blue coat.

For spring parade and graduation, we wore *Whites*. The white jacket was designed like the greens but made of white cotton linen. The pants were so starched that they nearly stood by themselves.

The uniforms were custom tailored unless you bought them used. The cadets donated their uniforms to the school at the end of the school year, and the school would resell them for a small profit. I bought used uniforms every year, and my Uncle Tony made whatever adjustments were necessary. They actually looked good. The only things that I bought new were my hat, shirts, and ties.

One week before school started, we reported to the armory to learn to drill and take care of our rifles. The seniors had just received their officer ranking, and they were gung-ho. While most adults had trouble with managing authority, seventeen-year-old kids were monsters. They acted like Paris Island drill sergeants. I wanted to say, *This is high school, asshole, lighten up!* Instead, I remembered how much this was costing, and I didn't want to get expelled before I started.

August is a miserable weather month. It was like Africa, 90-plus degrees and 90 percent humidity. The first few days we wore our street clothes, and then we switched to uniforms. Wearing wool in August—what foresight!

We reported at nine each morning. After three hours of close-order drill, learning to salute, learning the manual of arms, and listening to seventeen-year-old tyrants trying to act as though they were preparing us for the landing at Normandy, we broke for lunch.

More bullshit. Two upperclassmen were assigned to each table of eight. We picked up our lunch cafeteria style, marched to the table, sat in unison, and started to eat.

"What do you think you're doing, mister?" a skinny twit with captain's bars leaned over and yelled in my face. My first thought was of how short a time this asshole would last in the neighborhood.

"I think it's called eating," I said.

"Did I give you permission to eat?"

"No!"

"No, what?"

"No, you didn't give me permission to eat."

"It's no, *sir*, plebe!"

"No, sir."

"I can't hear you."

"No, sir!"

"I still can't hear you."

"Nooooo, siiiiir."

"That's better."

This is really bad acting, I thought. This guy is the master of the cliché. I'm not even a duker and I could kill this guy.

"May I eat now, sir?"

"Yes, you may eat a square meal. Does anyone know what a square meal is?"

The only guy with his head shaved is sitting across the table. He raised his hand.

"Tinsel. Do you know?"

"Yes, sir" he snapped.

He started making angular movements with his fork. I already hated this guy.

"Everyone at the table will sit at attention, look straight ahead, and follow Tinsel's lead."

Oh, God, I prayed. Get me out of here.

Armory was fun. We were each assigned an M1 Garand rifle which we took apart, cleaned, and put back together weekly. It was interesting the first few times. Since we never shot it, I could never figure why it required such care. It weighed 9.5 pounds, which doesn't sound like much unless you carry it on your shoulder for three hours.

In retrospect, this orientation week was actually very effective. It gave us plebes the opportunity to make friends quickly, to learn our way around the school, and to hear stories about teachers and their quirks. By the end of the week, the upperclassmen got all the military bullshit out of their system and turned out to be regular guys. Attending a military school where everyone goes home each night is different than boarding. By dinnertime, everyone is back into street clothes with their families. Although we wore our uniforms every day, the military only consisted of our weekly drills and morning inspections. We snapped to attention in class and marched to assembly; otherwise, it was relatively informal. No saluting in the hallways or harassment except for the first week of school when we were still learning the ropes.

The regiment consisted of two battalions and nine companies including the band. Each company had two platoons, each of which consisted of four squads. Each squad was comprised of six to eight cadets.

The school was part of the U.S. Army's Junior ROTC program and, as a result, required a periodic audit by the Army. The school was assigned a full bird colonel, who was responsible for maintaining the program standards. His title was PMS&T or Professor of Military Science and Tactics. He taught the classes and tested us periodically. Rank was awarded on the basis of the score achieved on these tests plus regular academic grades, minus any demerits earned.

Demerits were given primarily for failing part or all of inspection, i.e., shoes not shined, hair too long, belt buckle not shined, or pants or shirt not pressed. Demerits were also given for bad behavior such as insubordination. In addition to adversely affecting rank, demerits had to be worked off. Marching around the flagpole in front of the school for twenty minutes, euphemistically referred to as "guard duty," was the punishment for each demerit. For example, failing inspection was fifteen demerits or five hours of guard duty. It was very motivating not to screw up.

In lieu of physical education, we had a weekly three-hour drill. Regardless of the weather, every Thursday, immediately after lunch, we assembled on the grass behind the school. We marched into the armory, picked up our pieces, and reassembled on the road.

On warm, fair days we drilled on the grass behind the school. In the winter or on rainy days, we marched in the street through the city park to the Washington Avenue Armory. It was a good two miles. It was quite a sight—four hundred cadets with the band playing, stopping traffic, moving though the streets with disciplined perfection. The city people, those who were not late for appointments, loved it.

In spite of our heavy woolen overcoats and gloves, it was painfully cold. The fingers grabbing the butt of the rifle were always numb, and the colder the day, the heavier the rifle felt. One of the greatest motivations for rank was dumping the rifle. Officers carried swords and master sergeants carried holstered pistols. We resented the other really ritzy military school in town, Albany Academy, because they carried fake wooden rifles that only weighed a couple of pounds, and they rarely drilled in bad weather. *The benefit of being privileged*, I thought.

The Christian Brothers ran a disciplined, academically sound program. Located in over eighty countries throughout the world, it is a worldwide community of Brothers, numbering about 6600 today, and is headquartered in Rome, Italy. The United States/Toronto Region is "home" to more than 950 Brothers who serve in six Districts and the Delegation of Toronto. These Brothers serve in thirty states in the U.S. and in Toronto, in over 120 institutions, and work with nearly 80,000 students. The Order was much larger in the fifties and sixties.

The Brothers were not priests. They couldn't say Mass or administer the sacraments. They were a lay religious teaching order that took vows of poverty, chastity, and obedience.

The Brothers had three or four schools in New York State—two were military, two regular, and one reform school. The Brothers would rotate from school to school. We generally got the Brothers from the reform school. It was located in Barrytown, New York. It closed about twenty years ago and was sold to the "Moonies," that crazy Korean cult.

The Brothers, especially the reform school guys, were very much into corporal punishment. It is not an exaggeration to state that at least one kid was getting hit each hour of the school day. The hit could consist of a simple slap in the face to getting tossed around the classroom. Nobody complained because it was accepted as one of the methods of building character. Occasionally, something in excess would occur. For example, Brother Anthony, alias Freddy, was upset with Andy P. After Freddy put Andy P's head through the classroom door window, Freddy was quietly transferred.

My introduction to all this occurred on the first day of school. Brother William, who I later found out was one of the recent reform school transferees, was my homeroom teacher. He was a short, muscular type with blond hair who, in another time, could have easily passed for one of Hitler's youths. Homeroom was the first and last period of the day. It was to be used for study or homework. Brother William walked into class.

"Good morning, I am Brother C. William," he announced and wrote on the board simultaneously. "This is homeroom, and there will be no talking." He opened his briefcase, sat down, and started to read.

I turned to my new friend Tom S and said, "Now, there's a man of few words."

Brother looked up, calmly took off his watch. He stood up, and walked to my desk.

Looking at my name tag, "Cusato. Did I pronounce that right?" he smiled.

"Yes, Brother, perfect."

Effortlessly, he grabbed me by the shirt and lifted me off my seat.

"I said, 'No talking,'" he repeated with his face two inches from mine.

Totally void of emotion, he began slapping me as if he were hitting a speed bag. He hit me to the back of the room and then turned me and hit me back into my seat. It happened so fast that I was startled. All I remember is my face heating up as though I had just stuck it in an oven.

I was so disoriented that I blurted out, "What the fuck…?"

Instantly, another slap, "No talking includes profanity."

Walking backwards toward his seat, he continued, "While we're making friends, your hair is too long and fix your pants. Pegged pants are not what you were issued. I'll expect that to be done by tomorrow morning."

What a remarkable experience. I wasn't mad. I wasn't even scared. I actually kind of liked the guy. That night, my Uncle Tony fixed my pants, and my grandfather gave me a haircut.

My mother asked, "Well, how was your first day of school?"

"Not bad, Ma. Not bad," I said reflectively. I still couldn't explain my feelings.

Brother William and I became friends.

The Brothers were excellent teachers. At the beginning of each class there was a ten-question quiz. It was based on what was taught the day before. Eight percent of the grade was based on the daily quizzes. It worked because it forced you to study a little every day. To this day I have retained a tremendous amount of information, which I attribute to that method of teaching.

We all quickly learned the system. As we became more comfortable, we also learned the behavioral quirks of the Brothers and then the fun began.

At that time, the Brothers didn't use their real names. They used an initial and a first name, i.e., Brother A. Jerome or C. William. For some unknown reason, there were plenty of Williams and Anthonys. Most of the Brothers were pretty normal. There were a few with feminine man-nerisms; however, they behaved themselves. I never heard a story of any of them making a move on a student. If it happened, it was kept very quiet.

My theory was that all the repressed sexuality was manifested by their aggressive use of corporal punishment. The problem was that some were in control and others were out of control. One of the Brother Anthonys, I'm not sure which letter, whose nickname was "the fairy," taught English literature. He was artsy or, as some would say, a little light on his feet. We would torment him by making animal noises while he was writing on the blackboard. He would turn quickly and we would stop. Eventually, he would lose it.

Tinsel, whom I mentioned earlier, was a real military type. He shaved his head. His movements were jerky and stiff. He had the sense of humor of a dishrag. He would be the kind of officer that eventually would get shot by his own men. Tinsel sat in front of me in Anthony's class. Tinsel never acted up and was always a most attentive student. I could never distract him no matter how much I bugged him. Kevin, Jim, Dan, and I were the class disrupters. I would bend down behind Tinsel and make these animal noises. Brother turned, his eyes crazed.

"Whatever sneak is making those noises, I suggest you stop immedi-ately."

Not a sound was heard as he turned back to the board to write.

"Hoo hoot hoo hoot," we started again.

He turned again. This time, he grabbed a window pole that was rest-ing in the corner. A window pole is this 6-foot pole with a hook on the end that was used to open the large windows.

"It that you, Tinsel?"

He lifted the pole like an ax and bopped Tinsel right on the top of his shaved head.

It was the first time that I ever heard a cartoon sound in real life—boing! Tinsel didn't move. Brother turned back to the board and started writing again. Tinsel grabbed his head, started rubbing it back and forth very fast, while making painful facial expressions.

Brother turned back to the class again.

Tinsel immediately stopped, sat at attention at his desk while looking straight ahead. It was a sight. We used all our self-control to stop from falling on the floor in laughter.

Tinsel was a real soldier.

Brother Conrad had that real medieval monk look. He taught religion. He was best described as being bony. The skin was stretched over every feature in his face like a Halloween mask. He was tall, thin, and had a hand like a rock. He had staccato movements—quick and sharp.

Hoping that he would forget to give out a homework assignment, we wasted time in class by asking idiotic theological questions. He hated them. A few examples of the more common were:

"Brother, if God is all powerful can he make a rock so heavy that he can't lift it?"

"If God is all-knowing, can he make a square circle?"

This morning's topic was making your Easter duty. The good Brother was explaining that it was a mortal sin if you missed confession and didn't receive Communion before the end of Lent. I raised my hand.

"Brother, if I were on a cruise ship, and it was Easter Sunday, and we were about to cross the international dateline, and just as I was about to go to confession, the priest had a heart attack; suddenly the ship hit an iceberg and sank. This is my question. Would I go to heaven?"

With catechism in hand, he walked directly to my desk. He stared down on me as if he were about to explode. Instead, in a quiet, controlled voice he said, "Go out into the hallway and stand under the clock. I *will* be there directly after class. I strongly suggest that you pray that the clock falls on you before I get there."

I got up and walked into the hallway and stood under the large clock that hung from the ceiling. I waited. The period bell rang. Brother Conrad approached me. My eyes closed and my face wrinkled in anticipation of one of his famous slaps.

Instead he whispered, "If your intention was to make your Easter duty, I am sure God would forgive your procrastination."

Relieved, I said, "Oh, thank you, Brother, I *will* remember that." I turned and started back to class.

"One more thing," Brother grabbed my arm and turned me. In one fluid motion, he hit me with a slap that silenced the noise in the hall. My cheek felt as if it had been touched by a blowtorch.

"*That* is so you're not disappointed!" He walked into the faculty lounge. I staggered down the hall to my next class.

Brother Conrad was definitely born five hundred years too late!

13

One Down, Three to Go

I survived my freshman year with a few cuts and bruises, but I was definitely a changed person. My world quadrupled in size and in awareness and wisdom. I was almost fifteen and feeling my oats. I had made a gang of new friends with different names and different values. They spoke differently and dressed differently. I was slowly changing from a street kid to a preppy.

My buddies in the neighborhood were okay with me as long as I wasn't wearing my uniform. In fact, walking home on a snowy winter's day was like running the gauntlet. They would be waiting for me with snowballs. My hat was the perfect target. But it was now summer and time to make some money.

I worked a paper route from the time I was about twelve. I had sixty papers on the route, which I delivered six days per week. In those days there were two newspapers in town, the *Times Union,* a morning and Sunday paper, and the *Knickerbocker News,* the evening paper. I didn't want to get up earlier than I had to so I chose the *Knickerbocker News* to deliver.

It was a relatively easy job. A truck would come by about 3:30 in the afternoon and drop off my bundle. I cut the bundle and put the papers in a canvas bag with a padded shoulder strap. Once you memorized the route, and learned how to fold and throw a newspaper, it was an easy job. To fold it properly, you tucked the paper into itself, grabbed the edges of the tuck, pulled tight, and locked it by hitting the paper on your knee while bending it slightly. If it was done properly, the paper could be thrown thirty feet, hit the front door, and not open.

I was so efficient; I could deliver the entire route in thirty minutes. Fridays would take longer because it was collection day. It was forty cents per week. Most people would give me fifty and I'd keep the dime tip. My weekly bill was about $18. I collected from $24 to $30 and kept the difference. At Christmas, the paper would sell us these calendars for a quarter. We'd then give them to the customers hoping for a big tip. The average tip was $2. Some gave $5 and, some gave $1. Those who gave nothing would get a wet paper when it rained.

One of my customers was Gregorian's Grocery Store. It was a classical corner grocery store with a small deli that served Mediterranean and Italian specialties. Mr. Gregorian was this really nice Armenian guy. He was tall, paunchy with jet-black hair, and a nose the size of a small summer squash.

In the summer of '58, I quit my paper route for what I thought was my first real job: a grocery clerk for a dollar an hour. I didn't realize that as a paperboy I was an entrepreneur. I had no supervision and collected my money. I was a small business owner making three to six dollars per hour. Now I had to work six hours to make what took me two. Needless to say, even though I really liked Mr. Gregorian, stocking shelves and packing grocery bags didn't last very long.

About three weeks after I started working, I was at the Stuyvesant Shopping Center buying sneakers with my mom. Stuyvesant was one of the early outdoor strip malls. While she was in the dress shop, I wandered the Center. I noticed that a music store had just opened. It sold Hammond Organs. We had an organ at home, which I played reasonably well.

I walked into the store and started fooling around on one of the organs. Out of the back room came this big, burly guy with a blond crewcut and big toothy smile.

"Hi, there," he said with this Southern accent. "You play, do you?"

"Not well, I play chords and melody. You know, out of a fake book." I was a little intimidated by his size.

"Hi, my name is Barry. Barry Flower. My sister and I are the owners." He extended his hand.

I shook his hand. "You don't sound like you're from these parts." I got that line right out of a Hopalong Cassidy movie.

"Louisiana, Baton Rouge. We moved here for a little change of scenery. Why don't you play something?"

"No, I was just looking around. We have a Lowry at home," I said.

"Lowry's a good organ, but there's nothing like a Hammond. Come on, play something!"

I sat down and played a verse of "Moonglow," a great song for the organ.

"That was very good. Here, I've got something I think you'll like." We walked to the back to a glass walled room.

"This is Hammond's latest. It's called the Chord Organ. You play the keyboard with your right hand and with your left hand you press these chord buttons. The two pedals on the floor give you the first and the fifth for rhythm." He sat down and played "Chinatown."

He went on to show me the special sound effects like the banjo, trumpet, violin, and Hawaiian guitar.

"You get all this for only $995 plus $35 for the bench. You might want to tell your father about this."

"Actually, I was wondering if you needed any help around the store for the summer."

"Oh, we just might. How old are you?"

"Ah, sixteen." *I'll worry about proving that later*, I thought.

"Let me talk to my sister. Oh, what's your name?"

"Carl Cusato."

"That's 'I'talian isn't it?"

"Right, 'I'talian!"

"Leave me your telephone number, and I'll call you by tomorrow. You do have a sport jacket and tie, don't you?"

"Ah, oh yes."

I gave him my number, shook his hand, and left to meet my mother.

The next day I received a call offering me a job selling the Chord Organ. He would pay me $1.75 per hour plus $80 for every organ that I sold. Initially, I was really excited until I realized that I had never sold anything before nor had I ever played in public. I then became terrified.

I went to work that day and told Mr. Gregorian about the new job. He was happy for me but sad that I was leaving. He gave me some fruit to take home to my mother. What a good guy!

The next day I got ready for the new job. My only sport coat was a maroon and black, large hounds-tooth check that my Uncle Tony made me for my birthday for mowing his lawn for free. I wore black gabardine pants and shell cordovan loafers. My Aunt Josephine worked at the Cluett-Peabody Factory and gave me a bunch of Arrow shirts. My favorite was the white one with the tab collar. I wore a black, one-inch knit tie. I looked at least nineteen.

Getting to work was another problem. I took the Second Avenue bus downtown to State and Pearl, then I transferred to the Western Avenue bus whose route ended at Stuyvesant Plaza. It took about an hour, a twenty—five-cent student bus token, and a free transfer.

When I arrived at the store, Barry and his sister Daisy (I know Daisy Flower is hard to believe) met me with a very warm welcome. They told me how great I looked and how excited they were that I was joining them. It made me feel good even though I still had butterflies.

They told me that I would be training for the first week. I was to learn about six songs and learn how to demonstrate the instrument. I could dress casually during my training. The hourly rate could be treated as a draw against commissions so that they could pay me off the books and save me the taxes. I was too naïve to know what that meant. *Boy, are these nice people,* I thought.

By the end of the week I was pretty good, although sick of playing and talking. I must have repeated the sales pitch over a hundred times. I played the songs so much that I was playing them in my dreams. I learned these songs:

- "I'm Looking Over a Four-leaf Clover" to attract attention.
- "O, Susannah," to demo the banjo.
- "When the Saints Come Marching In," to demo the trumpet.
- "76 Trombones," for the trombone effect.
- "Elegy," to demo the violin, and
- "Hawaiian Wedding Song," for the Hawaiian guitar.

The following week I dressed up, boarded the bus, and headed to the office with great anticipation. On the way to work that day, I realized that I had neglected to ask where I was going to work. I initially assumed that I would work out of the store, but now, for some reason, I had my doubts. Why would they train me for week so intensely when I could train on the job? The mystery was soon to be solved.

When I arrived at the store, Barry was ready for me. The Chord Organ was already loaded into the Van and a stack of sales literature was on the counter.

"Well, here's our star," Barry and Daisy greeted me with a big smile. "Are you ready for your 'baptism of fire'?"

"It depends. Where are we going?"

"You'll love this. You are going to make a lot of money."

"How so?"

"I made a deal with A&P Supermarkets. As part of a promotional tie-in, we get to demo the Chord Organ. The customer enters the contest to win one as a prize at the end of the contest, and we get to follow up with people who are interested. Isn't that great?"

"You mean I'm going to sell organs in a grocery store?"

"A supermarket!"

"Won't I scare people? After all, people are there to buy food and suddenly they hear this organ."

"It's perfect. You'll be a big hit."

"Shit, I just quit my job at the market a week ago."

"You'll love it. You'll change markets every two days. There are ten participating. Don't worry, I'll be there to get you started."

I picked up the literature and headed for the van. I opened the door and there wasn't a passenger's seat.

"Where do I sit?"

"Oh, we got the basic model." He slid over a wooden box. "Sit on this." He put a towel over the box it so I wouldn't get my pants dirty.

I got in and off we went to the A&P. We pulled up to the delivery entrance and opened the rear doors. He took these tracks out of the van and pulled the organ onto the delivery dock. The organ had wheels, and we rolled it into the store. The manager met us and directed us to the frozen food area. I brought in the bench and set up the contest signs.

"Well, that looks pretty good. Is there anything else you need?" Barry said with one foot out the door.

"Yeah, a paper bag for my head."

"Watch! I'll show you how easy it is."

He sat down, turned up the volume, and started playing. Sure enough, people started gathering around. When he had a crowd, he turned and started the sales pitch.

> "Welcome, Ladies and Gentlemen, to the Hammond Organ and A&P summer promotion. What you see before you is the latest in musical instrumental advancement (they didn't use the word technology in those days), the Hammond Chord Organ. So advanced, so simple it virtually plays itself. No need for talent. No need for experience. Our color-coded keyboard and numbered chord buttons enables even those without any previous musical experience to play almost instantly. With our many musical voices, you can play the sound of the banjo, trumpet, trombone, and even the Hawaiian guitar."

After demonstrating the sounds, he grabbed someone from the audience, usually a young kid or older person, and had them play "Silent Night" following the colors on the chart and keyboard.

He then asked for people to sign up for the free record of organ music.

After watching him, I felt much better. *The people loved it. I can do that,* I thought.

When he finished, he got up, looked at me, and said, "You're on your own, kid," and left. My heart sank.

I was really nervous the first time, but as the day progressed I became more relaxed and confident. I just repeated the pitch that I had memorized and played my six songs. Music is really powerful. I watched how it mesmerized people. By the end of the day I had collected almost fifty names of people who wanted a free record. When Barry picked me up at eight, I couldn't stop talking.

The next day I almost swaggered into the market. About 4:00 PM the frozen food manager came by, "Hey kid, I don't want to hurt your feelings, but don't you know any other songs? Those songs over and over again are driving me crazy."

Two days was long enough in each market. In fact, two days was long enough for me, period. Playing eight hours a day is grueling. After the first week, I was getting buggy. In spite of meeting a few good-looking girls, I realized how hard this work really was.

I gave Barry all my leads, and he and Daisy went through them and picked out the best ones. I didn't know the criteria other than good neighborhoods and money to buy.

We played two locations the first week. With almost one hundred leads, we spent the next week following up. I sat in the van on the wooden box while he looked for nice houses.

I rang the bell and introduced myself.

"Hi, do you remember me? We met at the A&P last week. I was the crazy guy playing the organ in the frozen food department." If they remembered, I continued.

"You signed up for a free organ record, and since we were in the neighborhood, I thought we'd save the postage and give it to you personally."

We continued with a little more small talk.

"You know, maybe you could help us out, and have some fun at the same time. My boss just got a large shipment of Chord Organs, and we have temporarily run out of storage space. If we could store one in your living room, you'd do us a big favor. All we ask is that you treat it like one of your pieces of fine furniture. We'll give you a free lesson and instruction book. It's only for a week, no cost, no obligation!"

I couldn't believe that people actually said yes. We then backed up the van to the front door and rolled that thing right in the living room. Barry would give them a lesson and off we went.

One week later Barry set up an appointment and closed the deal. This guy was really good at closing.

I received my first commission the first week. Four brand new $20 bills. *This was the big time,* I thought. I finished playing in the rest of the stores and over the next month we placed about twenty organs. My sport jacket was getting worn out, and my pants were getting shiny from daily wear and pressing.

He only paid for four sales. When I asked him about it, he told me that the others didn't close or were pending. Over the summer, I made friends with the warehouse guys who moved the equipment and handled deliveries. One Friday near the end of the summer, I saw one of them on the bus on the way home. He confidentially told me that they had sold the organs and just hadn't paid me.

The next evening I confronted Barry.

"I heard that you sold more organs and didn't pay me."

"Who told you that?"

"I checked with the customers. I had their numbers."

"You calling me a liar. Do you think I'd cheat you?"

"No, I'm just asking," I said nervously.

"Well, I was going to give it to you next Tuesday after Labor Day, your last day at work…and a little bonus. Now, you've ruined the surprise."

I felt bad that I had questioned him, but I was so excited, I ran to the bus. On the way home, I was counting the money in my mind. I figured maybe $1,000. I'd pay my tuition, buy a new uniform, and give the rest to my mother. Labor Day weekend was filled with family picnics and just hanging out with friends.

On Tuesday, I arrived at the store about 11 AM. To my shock, the store was closed.

There was a truck in the back loading the inventory.

"Hey, buddy, what's going on?" I asked the driver.

"Who are you?" he said, not lifting his head from the clipboard.

"I work here."

"No more, pal. Your boss didn't pay his bills. We're repossessing the merchandise."

"Where is he?"

"Don't know. I heard someone saw them leaving with a U-haul."

"He can't leave. He owes me money," I shouted.

"Yeah, yeah, stand in line." He rolled up the window

I walked slowly back to the bus stop. I boarded the bus and sat in the rear seat. As hard as I tried, I couldn't stop from crying. I had already spent the money in my mind. All I could think of were the hours playing at the supermarket and how I just got screwed. I didn't know whether I was hurt or mad.

I felt like a little kid.

14

CYO and Artsy-Fartsy

The Catholic Youth Organization was a social/service club that the Church set up to get us teenagers off the street and so we could socialize with other Catholic youth. In those days, getting married outside the religion was a big deal so they tried to control the situation early. It was a coed thing, something to do on a Sunday night, and I made new friends, most of whom were two or three years older. This was particularly important because they could drive! Mobility suddenly became important.

We met in the St. James gym every Sunday night. We had a ten-minute meeting where I was first introduced to parliamentary procedure—a more civilized way of getting someone's attention than yelling or throwing something at him or her. I learned about motions and seconds and moving the previous questions and points of information. I was getting very sophisticated. I tried to use it with the street guys and it went nowhere. All I got was Louie grabbing his crouch and saying, "Move this!" Sadly, my worlds were drifting apart.

Immediately after the meeting, the records were turned on and we started dancing. We learned to dance by watching Dick Clark's American Bandstand, the show from Philadelphia that was on TV every day after school. We did the stroll, the twist, the cha-cha-cha, and the Bandstand version of the "Lindy." The best, of course, was the slow dance. The priest and nuns would walk around the dance floor to make sure that there was a space between the dancers. It was like trying to separate magnets. The minute they turned away, back together everyone would go.

A few months into the year I was elected Vice President of the Chapter. I didn't even run for the office. Someone must have written me in. I didn't have to do anything except sit at the head table and look as though I was interested and/or knew what I was doing. If the president died, I would be president. At fifteen, we didn't have many deaths in office.

I did get to go the National Convention in Buffalo. Father Murphy drove the four of us there in his Ford Fairlane. Being stuffed in that car over five hours was misery. When we got there, it was "goodie two shoe" heaven. I couldn't wait to get back to Second Avenue.

Later that year, the Diocese came up with the idea of the CYO doing a "Passion Play" that would be performed at the various parish schools during Lent. It was called "The Redeemer" and it was about the last days of Christ's life. Everyone was very excited and all the fruitcakes couldn't wait for the auditions. The play was to be directed by Mattie Symentza, a guy who was big in the local civic theater circuit and also active in the church.

Personally, I ignored the whole idea. I knew nothing about the theater and had no interest in learning.

The auditions were held at our school auditorium all day Sunday leading up to our CYO meeting. I made the colossal mistake that night of forgetting this fact and getting to the meeting early.

I stood in the back of the auditorium as unobtrusively as possible, and watched as the auditions came to a close. Unfortunately, Father Murphy and Father B were standing at the front watching the auditions and talking.

I must have been in a daze or daydreaming when suddenly I got this feeling someone was watching me. When I regained focus, I noticed

Father Murphy headed toward me down the right side of the gym, and Father B headed toward me down the left side of the gym. *It's a good time for a smoke,* I thought. As if I didn't notice them, I headed out the back door.

I made it to the stairwell and started up the first step when I felt the Father B's grip on my shoulder. I turned and there stood Father B and Murphy with shitty grins on their faces.

"Hey, Mr. Vice President, where are you going?" Father B asked.

"I was just going outside for a smoke," I replied.

"Aren't you going to audition?" Father Murphy joined in.

"For what?" Can't change old ways. Answer a question with a question when you smell trouble.

"Father Murphy and I were just talking about the role of the High Priest, Caiaphas. I was asking, who do we know that is dark, tall, and has a deep voice?"

"Billy Pedulla?" I was reaching.

Silence.

"Ritchie Noonan?" More pathetic desperation.

Silence.

"Excuse me, I have to go the bathroom." I started to walk to the bathroom when the vice grip descended upon my shoulder.

"We were thinking about you."

"Oh no, Father, you can forget about that."

"You're refusing to help. Did you forget why Jesus died for your sins?"

"So I could audition for his life story?"

"Try to stay healthy," his grip tightened.

"I'm not putting on a dress and makeup. Everybody will think I'm a fag."

"It's not a dress. They're vestments, like we wear for Mass. And it's not makeup, it's just a beard. It'll make you look older. You'll love it. You'll be the next Douglas Fairbanks. Father Murphy, will you assist me?"

With Father B on one arm and Father Murphy on the other, they escorted me to the front of the gym.

"Mattie, I think we found you a Caiaphas."

Mattie, sympathetic with my hijacking, was very kind. He came over to me and asked if I was all right with it. I motioned in a defeating way. He whispered that he would make it as painless a possible.

"Now repeat this line in as a commanding voice as possible." He had a real announcer's voice. "You have insufferable iteration! Now, out with it!"

I blew out the line. It definitely was loud and deep.

"Well, that ought to shake the pews at St. Catherine's," Mattie looked at the priests and started chuckling.

He looked back me and said, "Welcome aboard, Caiaphas."

"Is that all I have do?"

"That, and a few more lines, you'll be great. You've got nothing to worry about," he nonchalantly quipped.

How did this happen? I thought. What have I done? The priests were laughing and patting me on the back. As it turned out, I had more than "a few more lines." It was one of the larger parts in the play. We rehearsed every night from 6:30 to 9 PM. I got my copy of the script and highlighted all my lines. I read them over every day. I got my sister to read them with me.

After a few weeks, we were rehearsing without the scripts in hand. Everything was new to me. *Stage left, stage right, upstage, pronounce, project, proscenium* were new words and concepts as were the smells of cold cream and spirit glue. It seemed that we rehearsed forever. Along with the part came a certain respect from the other actors and people who worked behind the scenes. I liked the feeling. This was a much bigger deal than I ever imagined.

Opening night was traumatic. It finally hit me that I was going to do this before live people, alone, without a script to read. What would happen if I forgot the words or if I fell down? I'd be humiliated for life. How could I have said yes to this? I can't do it. Then, I started hoping the stage would catch on fire or there would be a storm and the electricity would go out.

I stood in costume looking in the mirror. I wore a maroon flowing garment and a full gray beard. My face had been darkened with makeup. I almost scared myself. I wasn't sure whether I had to pee or throw up.

Mattie came backstage and gave us a pep talk. I must have looked really bad, because he came over to me and whispered, "Break a leg." "Great idea," I replied. Smiling at my reaction, he said, "That means good luck in the theater."

The music began and the curtain rose, as did my breathing and blood pressure. I waited for my cue. Finally, I heard my line and walked onto the stage not knowing if any sound was going to come out of my mouth.

My first line was, "Where is this Jesus now?"

I took a deep breath and pounded the line. I heard the sound of my own voice as if I were listening to someone else. I was so tense that I was told that the whites of my eyes could be seen in the last row. Suddenly I wasn't scared anymore. It was as if I was shot with a drug. It was euphoric. Everything made sense. I not only knew what I was to say but what everyone on stage was about to say. I felt bigger than life. My voice projected as if it was attached to a microphone. I felt relaxed, even graceful. The two-hour three-act play ended in two minutes and three seconds...or so it seemed.

Finally the curtain fell, and we took our bows. What a great feeling of accomplishment and camaraderie. I had made it through it all without muffing a line or missing a cue. What a miracle!

The reviews were very good. Something extraordinary had happened to me, and I was hooked.

15

Coney Island Was a Bad Idea

The play was a big success. We had a party and celebrated our histrionic prowess. When you spend so much time with the same people striving for the same goal, it creates a lasting bond. Lines from the play regularly pop up and are integrated into normal conversation. The character that you play in a way stays attached and becomes part of how you are viewed by the group. A different persona began to evolve. It was as though Big Coose and Carlucci had passed on. My language was better. I was conscious of the sound of my voice. All this was occurring from one amateur theatrical experience.

However, I was being pulled. Each group of friends was so dramatically different that eventually there had to be casualties. I couldn't hold on to them all.

I started hanging around with the group from the play. Some of them were a few years older and had cars so that we could go to the drive-in movies, get ice cream, or buy beer. In New York, at that time, the drinking age was eighteen, which meant everyone started at fifteen.

One day the group decided to go to Coney Island. Richie G had a 1955 white Buick convertible. It was a beauty with room for six.

After getting permission, we scheduled to go on a Saturday. It was only 150 miles away so that we could leave early in the morning and return late the same day. The group was made up of Ritchie G, Mike S, Billy P, the Burtell twins, and me. I still remember what I wore—pair of white cotton pants, a turquoise shirt, and charcoal gray hushpuppy loafers.

We met at Ritchie's house about 6:30 in the morning. We packed some sandwiches, chipped in for gas. I was the first driver. In order to save money on tolls, we decided to take the Taconic Parkway rather than the NYS Thruway. The Taconic was narrower, and not as straight as the Thruway, but was very scenic. It was built in the '20s and was the main north/south highway in New York until the Thruway was finished in the '50s.

It was a cool, overcast May morning. We made it to the Taconic entrance in about thirty minutes. Six of us were packed tightly into the Buick. The radio was blasting our favorite rock and roll songs. Everything was good in the world.

About an hour and a half into the trip, I started to get stomach cramps. I loved to drive so much in those days that I tried to ignore them. Finally, I pulled over. It was starting to rain. I got out of the car and, for some unexplainable reason, instead of getting in the front passenger side I lifted the driver's seat and slid into the back. Billy P moved over to drive. Ritchie G moved to the middle, Mike S got out of the back and rode shotgun. My cramps gradually disappeared, and I fell into a deep sleep.

Suddenly, I felt myself floating and then I felt wet. I thought that I was dreaming. When I opened my eyes, I was sitting in a shallow swamp. The warm water barely covered my chest. I looked around and could see nothing but trees and bushes. I shook myself conscious and stood up. My shirt and pants were ripped and my shoes were missing. I heard sounds coming from the brush on my left. I pushed my way through to the other side. What I saw dropped me to my knees. I slapped myself to make sure that I was awake.

"This can't be happening," I whispered over and over.

There before me was a nightmare. Bodies were scattered all over the road. One car was turned on its side. The Buick was standing on its bumper resting on a tree. The convertible top had been ripped off, and the seats were scattered randomly on the highway. I heard a woman crying in the overturned car. I ran over, pulled her out, and rested her on the ground. I looked down and saw that her foot was only hanging by a tendon. I couldn't recognize anyone. There was blood all over the place. *I'd better call home*, I thought.

Barefoot, I started running down the highway. I arbitrarily picked a direction. Luckily, it was the right one. After about a mile, I saw a gas station. The rain was heavy, and I was soaked to the bone. I ran inside.

"I need to use your phone," breathing heavily.

"Pay phone is over there," the toothless attendant motioned.

"I don't have any money. May I use your regular phone? There's been a serious accident."

"Not suppose to…all right." He motioned for me to come behind the counter.

I looked up at the clock. It was about 10:30 AM. I picked up the phone and dialed home. My mother answered.

"Hi Mom! It's me. Look, there's been an accident. There's blood all over the place. I'm okay, call you later."

I hung up. In my nervousness, I neglected to tell her where, although as I think back, I didn't really know at the time where I was, other than near New York City.

To say that my mother was distraught was an understatement. She knew there had been an accident and that there was blood all over. She didn't know who was hurt or how badly or who was even alive. Worst of all, she didn't know where. "A fine mess," as Oliver Hardy would say.

As my mother described it later, the next few hours were hell. She had to call the other mothers to tell them of the accident, but could tell them no more. My father spent hours with the highway patrol trying to find out where the accident could have occurred.

Back at the gas station, I thanked the attendant and ran back to the scene. When I arrived, there were several ambulances, a fire truck, and several patrol cars. My buddies were already loaded into the ambulances and ready to leave for the hospital. I grabbed one of the drivers.

"Can you take me, too?"

"Who are you?"

"I was in the accident. I just went to make a call."

"Hey, doc, we have another one over here." The doctor ran over, checked my eyes and my other vitals.

"How do you feel? Anything hurt?" he asked.

"No," I said.

"You're a lucky guy. Get in. You can sit up front." We drove to the hospital with sirens blasting. Not a word was spoken.

At the emergency entrance, the ambulances backed into the docks and teams of emergency room workers came out and rushed the stretchers into the operating rooms. I got out, and watched as all five of my friends were taken off. I was still in shock and wasn't registering the severity of it all.

A young, pretty candy striper approached me and offered me a robe. I refused. She pointed out that I was "hanging out." I reached behind me, and realized that my pants and underwear had ripped and my fanny was on display. I took the robe.

I approached the nurse at the desk and asked about my friends.

"You were in the accident?" She asked.

"Yes."

"Has the doctor checked you?"

"At the site, he checked my eyes," I said.

"Wait right here."

The doctor came out, brought me into an examining room, and started a physical.

"How is everybody?" I asked.

He looked at me for a moment as if he was deciding how to tell me, "I'm sorry, one of your friends didn't make it."

My heart sank. No one my age had ever died before.

"Do you know his name?" I asked.

"No, we are waiting for confirmation from the family."

"I could…"

Interrupting, "I don't think that would be a good idea."

"What about the rest of the guys?"

"Everyone else will recover. A few broken bones, many stitches, and some ugly bruises." He continued examining me.

"Can I see them?"

"Let me finish checking you out and we'll see." He completed a very thorough check. He then led me to the recovery rooms.

There were three beds in one room and four in the other. Ritchie was in one of the beds. His face was almost completely wrapped, and his arm was cast in plaster. Bill was in the next bed: his nose was in a splint and his leg was in a cast. In the next bed was a person from the other car. In the next room were the Burtell twins. They were sleeping, but didn't look too banged up. The other two beds were people from the other cars.

The mystery had been solved. Mike S was dead. He sat "shot gun" or in the front passenger seat by the window. This was the seat that I should have moved to. *What made me get in the back?* I thought.

I walked out of the room in a daze. Even though I knew Mike the least of anyone in the car, the empty feeling was as though I lost a brother.

I wandered back to the lobby and I realized that I should call home. I found out from the nurse that we had been taken to Grasslands Hospital in Valhalla, New York, not far from White Plains. *Valhalla,* I thought, *isn't that where the Vikings go when they die?*

They put me in one of their customer service rooms to make the call. My father answered.

"Dad, is that you?"

"Are you all right, Son?"

"Yeah, I'm fine. We're at Grasslands Hospital."

"Yeah, we know. I have been tracking you down for the past several hours. We appreciated your call, but next time be a little more specific. Your mother is a mess. I guessed, given the time, that you must have been around White Plains."

"Is she there?"

"She and the other mothers left in the station wagon about ten minutes ago. Mike's family is going down separately."

"So you know."

"Unfortunately."

"Well, see you later, Dad."

"Son?"

"Yeah?"

"I love you."

"Me too, Dad." I hung up and started to cry. The harder I tried to hold it back, the harder I cried. I balled like a baby. It felt good.

I regained my composure and walked back out into the hallway. Two state troopers were sitting at a table, writing the accident report.

Curious about what exactly happened, I walked over and introduced myself.

"Are you reporting on the accident on Taconic Parkway this morning involving the six kids in the Buick?"

"Yes, how can I help you?"

"Well, I was a passenger in the back, but fell sleep and didn't really see what happened."

"You must be the missile who landed in the swamp."

"Yes, that's where it started for me. What happened?"

The trooper began reading and commenting.

"From what we can piece together, the south-bound Buick jumped the median and landed in the north-bound lane where it hit several cars traveling north. We are guessing that you hit an oil slick. The group of women traveling behind you reported that the car flipped forward, catapulting whoever was sitting in the back over a 10-foot hedge. I assume that was you. The others were thrown onto the oncoming cars or onto the pavement. You must have been wearing your pixie dust."

The trooper smiled and continued writing.

Well, that story gave me pause. I walked back into the recovery room to see how the guys were doing. They were conscious but obviously drugged. They were happy to see me and, of course, I was happy they were alive. I mentioned the mothers were on their way, but did not mention Mike.

It was evening, and I was suddenly hungry. The nurse told me that the employee cafeteria was on the lower level. I borrowed a few dollars from her and walked down three flights. The elevator wasn't working. Unfortunately, my walk took me past the door to the morgue. An unpleasant chill momentarily struck me. Finally, I reached the cafeteria. It was quiet with only one gentleman eating by himself. I ordered a couple of hot dogs and a Coke.

Meanwhile, the mothers arrived. When my mother couldn't find me, she began to panic. No one knew what happened to me. Finally, the nurse who loaned me the money returned to her station and directed her to the cafeteria.

She also must have enjoyed her walk past the morgue. She arrived at the cafeteria, her purse in hand, emotionally rattled. She had been riding in a car for three hours with three other mothers with injured sons. I can only imagine how sliceable the tension must have been.

She ran across the cafeteria, crying. I got up, my mouth full of hot dog, and got a big hug.

We talked a few minutes. She was definitely glad to see me. About an hour later we got back into the station wagon and returned home. I slept in the back.

To this day I have never seen Coney Island.

16

Hey, Bennie, Don't Beat Me

The Coney Island accident was an emotionally draining event. Mike's funeral was very sad. Ritchie and Billy had this religious epiphany and decided to join the priesthood. Unfortunately, seminary life wasn't that exciting, and the prospect of never getting laid again soon dissolved their religious vocation. They were out in six months. I hate to sound cynical but those lifelong lasting decisions can't be made on an emotional basis. I felt blessed that I had been saved, but I took it as God's way of saying, "Keep up the good work." Before that statement is misunderstood, allow this clarification: "I am sincerely thankful."

Summer was coming and I needed a "no-brainer" job. No organs or supermarkets this time. A friend of mine had been working at a day camp as a counselor. He said the owner was a good guy and it was fun. It was an eight to five, Monday to Friday schedule, leaving the evenings and weekends open for summer fun.

The owner was the principal of Schuyler High School, named after Phillip Schuyler of Revolutionary War fame. Schuyler was in the toughest area of town, and Ben Becker ran the school with an iron hand. One of the only true Jewish dukers that I ever met, Ben looked as tough as he was. In his early sixties, he stood about five-eight, had a bullish, muscular frame, and was completely bald. He had been a boxer in his youth and his face reflected it. He was extremely knowledgeable about the sport and was appointed the team manager for the 1960

Olympic boxing team that included Cassius Clay. Some thought that he was more knowledgeable than the coach.

Ben was also a great businessman. He bought several acres of land in Guilderland, an Albany suburb. He developed the land and converted it into a day camp for kids from six to thirteen. He had a beautiful wife who was either Kirk Douglas's sister or sister-in-law. I never got the story right.

Camp Nassau was the antithesis of his high school. While Schuyler High consisted of tough, mostly black, inner-city kids, the camp focused mainly on upscale, white Jewish kids. As tough as he was with the inner city kids, he was equally gentle with his camp kids. The counselors were another story.

My friend Richard got me the interview. I met Ben in his office at the camp a few weeks before it officially opened. The male counselors already were working, painting, cutting grass, and fixing up the facilities. He looked me over, asked me a few questions about school, grades, and family, and hired me on the spot.

He gave me a long lecture on safety and my responsibility for keeping the kids from getting hurt. This was a very serious subject with him. He told me the pay was fifty dollars a week or seventy-five if I drove a bus. Not only was I too young to drive the bus, but after Coney Island, I had no interest in driving anything or anyone but myself.

There were all kinds of stories about Ben. He was notoriously very tough with the counselors. He had a broken pinky that stuck out when he talked. The legend was when he bent back his pinky that was a sign that he was about to hit you. Later in the year, when I knew him better, we were horsing around after camp closed. Arnie Slager was a counselor from New York City and a college student. I think Ben was a friend of his family. Ben was showing us some boxing moves.

"Oh, so you're a lefty."

"Yeah, watch out," I joked.

"Keep that right up and look in my eyes." He started to circle.

He faked a left and slapped me in the face with a right.

"You're not looking!"

He did it again, then again.

"Okay, that's enough." He grabbed my head and messed up my hair.

"I know the rumor, but I would never hit you guys. If I hit Arnie, being a Jew, he'd sue me. If I hit you, being Italian, you'd hit back or wait five years, come back, and hit me when I am in a wheelchair. You're slightly a better candidate. Either way it doesn't pay."

He had a great sense of humor.

He introduced me to the other counselors who were working the grounds. There were two college kids from out of town who lived in a cabin on the grounds, two high school seniors, and two young schoolteachers. From what I could tell, I was the youngest. They were all very friendly.

The next morning I hitched a ride with one of the local guys. It was hot, and Bennie worked us hard all day. I was sent down to the lake to paint the boat shack, get all the life jackets cleaned up and fixed, and check the rowboats and canoes. Just the kind of thing a city kid like me knew volumes about.

The lake was really just a big pond. It had a muddy bottom and algae. Who knew what was growing and living in it. It gave me the willies when I had to get in the water and walk in the mud.

The counselors had two types of jobs: a tribal chief or an activity manager. It seemed that all summer camps had this thing about Indians. I always thought the Indian thing was pretty boring. Each age group was divided into tribes by gender.

For example, the ten-year-old boys were called "Sioux" and the ten-year-old girls were called "Herons." As a tribal chief, the counselor stayed with his group the whole day as they would travel from activity to activity and act as a teacher/baby-sitter. An activity manager stayed in one area and the kids were brought to him. Activity manager was the best job.

Since I fixed up the lake at pre-camp, I petitioned and got the lake job. Because the camp had a big pool and the lake was so slimy, the only thing the tribes would come down for were the rowboats and canoes. Of course, after I had carefully spread the rumor that a water snake had been seen, many tribes skipped the lake, making it the laziest job at the camp.

All was not perfect. The lake was in a gully and, as a result, was hot and had mosquitoes.

I wasn't totally comfortable. When the tribes did come down, I put everyone in life jackets, put them in the boats in pairs, and let them row around for forty-five minutes.

Each tribe had two CIT (counselors-in-training). They were fourteen-year-old beauties that helped out the counselors. They didn't get paid because they were in training but learning to be counselors—a clever way to get free help. They would give me back rubs during the period. Unfortunately, Mrs. Becker busted me, and that ended in about a week. I had this job almost the entire summer. When one of the counselors got sick, I had to fill in as a tribal chief.

I was assigned the Iroquois, the thirteen-year-old boys. They weren't street-kid thirteen but pampered Jewish thirteen, or emotionally nine and book-smart sixteen. The campers had already named me "Cool Carl, the lake guy," so winning them over wasn't difficult. These were the true veterans of the day camp. Most of them hated it. They had been campers for more than five years. They didn't want to make any belts or head gear. They just wanted to hang out and bug the younger kids.

At the end of the summer the campers put on a show. They would sing songs and act out things. It was usually pretty lame but it was tradition, and it was a mark that summer was ending. Each tribe had to come up with a show. There would be a competition and each year a plaque was made and hung in the "rec" building with the winner's name. The Iroquois never won. No one was ever able to get these cynical thirteen-year-olds motivated.

"West Side Story" was a big hit on Broadway. The movie was being made and everyone knew the songs, especially these kids. I suggested that we could do a camp parody on the story. They loved the idea of being gang members. Instead of the "Sharks," we'd be the "White Fish." I played the guitar in those days, so I wrote the parodies on the bus to and from the camp each day, and we rehearsed for the next two weeks—a good excuse to stay out of the sun.

The first parody was to "Officer Krupke." I remember the first verse:

> *Officer Becker to camp we have come*
> *With the dumb idea that it's ours to run*
> *We talk during Showtime, make all kinds of noise*
> *That's cause we all are very poised.*
> *We are poised, we are poised, we are all so poised...*

On the poised line, the entire tribe would do a Jerry Lewis impression. They all loved being hams. I told them the bigger the better. They'd wander the stage and then snap back into formation for the next verse. They thought it was so funny that they loved rehearsing it.

I needed a song that described the counselors. Instead of a West Side Story song, I used the old Louie Prima, Italian favorite "Hey Marie," and changed it to "Hey Bennie." Here's the first verse,

Hey, Bennie, don't beat me
Is a song all our counselors sing
He makes them potzo (crazy)
Instead of water
He gives them matzos

We won the competition. For the next few weeks, the whole camp was singing the songs. Ben loved it and offered me a job the next summer.

He didn't even get mad when I was caught the next summer, late one night, skinny-dipping with the synchronized swimmer from Toronto who was visiting Ben's family.

17

The Legend of Whip Willie

With all the distractions in my life, I still gravitated to the neighborhood. The bus from the camp dropped me off about six. I ate dinner and wandered outside. There was always someone sitting on the porch or hanging out at Barbaro's. A few of the guys had cars so there was always something to do. When the carnival was in town, we hung out there.

The Church had a big, four-day festival with rides, plenty of food, and gambling. It was amazing. They had roulette, games with big dice, the birdcage on the wheel, and blackjack. The minimum bet was a quarter and the max was two dollars. I guess gambling is legal when the Catholic Church is in charge of the political lobbying. Nobody talked about the fact that it drew gamblers from all over the city. There was even talk of after-hours, big money games held in the garages behind the church during the festival. Netting fifty or sixty thousand in four days is no amateur undertaking.

Drive-in movies were the rage. There must have been ten of them within a ten-mile radius. We either went with a car full of guys or we double-dated. When they charged by the head, we packed three in the trunk. Those '50s cars had what we called "mafia trunks." They could hold three bodies comfortably. Eventually they started charging by the car and hiding in the trunk didn't matter. We bought a bunch of food and few six-packs and sat on the hood or roof, watched the movies, or harassed the lovers.

When we double-dated, we brought some beer and necked for two hours. You could always tell who was necking by the steam on the windows. After two hours, your mouth would actually hurt. Still, the drive-in was definitely a place where you got to know someone better.

When things were slow, we went downtown to the dives. The Grand Tavern and the Orange Street Grill were our regular first stops. These were the bars of the derelicts. It was rumored that they even advertised in the *National Dump Pickers Review*. There were long wooden bars right out of the last century and a few tables and booths. They had a dart board and a coin-operated bumper pool table. They served pickled hard-boiled eggs, Slim Jims, chips, and nuts. Nothing else was safe to eat. We liked going there because they believed our phony proof and after a few visits they didn't even check.

There was always a sideshow. Mostly working guys and a few "over the hill" hookers made up the usual crowd. There was a jukebox that played rhythm and blues and the old standards.

It was actually pretty safe. The bartenders were old longshoremen who never let anything get out of hand. We showed up, drank a few beers, had a few laughs with the hookers, and left. It wasn't about drinking. It was about macho.

It was a warm August evening. Nothing exciting was going on so Dirty Hands, Louie, and Clods thought it might be a good idea to make the rounds. I had mixed feelings going out with these guys. On the one hand, they were great fun and great fighters so I felt safe. On the other, trouble had a way of following them. We got into Louie's '54 Ford and headed downtown.

It was about eight o'clock when we walked into the Grand. The place was dead—a few old guys at the bar and one sleeping in the booth. We ordered a Schafer beer and drank it out of the bottle. We stayed about ten minutes and left. Two blocks down the street was the Orange Street Grill, so we decided to walk.

Orange Street was jumping. Construction workers, bikers, or just street people, it was hard to tell. It was certain that they were not members of the local polo team. Compared to Dirty Hands, Louie, and Clods, I looked like a baby. At sixteen I was nearly six feet tall, but thin and with no prospect of a beard. They had been shaving since they were twelve. They were bigger and more muscular. They could easily pass for twenty or more. Although they would deny it, they loved to fight.

The minute that we walked in, I could feel that something was going to happen. We walked to the end of the bar to the only empty space available. We ordered some Schafers, leaned back and looked around, trying to look cool and confident. There were a couple of guys and their girls dancing to some "doo wop" songs from the jukebox. Two or three more guys were playing bumper pool and darts. Everyone seemed to be having a good time. There was nothing to worry about. Why then was my upper lip starting to quiver? Whenever I was close to trouble, my upper lip would involuntarily start to quiver, not noticeably but I could feel it.

I turned to the guys and suggested that we leave to get a pizza. Out of the corner of my eye, I saw Clods talking to some girl. Then, completely out of nowhere, it started: *pop, pop, pop!* Punches were being thrown. Bottles were flying. The place was in chaos. It happened so fast that I was stunned. I took two steps and slid down behind the bar. All I could think of was how to get out. Just then a hand reached down and grabbed me by the shirt and pushed me out from behind the bar. It was the bartender.

"Get out of here," he said. He had a bat in his left hand.

Just as I got up I felt a fist hit me right in the chest. It knocked me back to the wall.

Just then a guy came flying by and hit the wall next to me. Dizzy from the punch, he looked right at me. He was a tall skinny guy. I thought if I were going to hit anyone, it ought to be a skinny guy. I wound up, just as I saw in the movies, and hit him right on the jaw. He went down. **Wow**, I thought. *It worked.* He went down just like he was supposed to go down.

Within five seconds the pain flew up my arm. It was so excruciating that I could feel my eyes watering. I never had really hit anyone before. The fights that I had in the past were wrestling matches with a few love taps. This was a full-blown hit, and it hurt. It really hurt. As I held my hand, reeling from the pain, this gorilla grabbed me.

"That was my brother you sucker punched," he said as his big hairy paw cocked back ready to put me in "la-la" land. Just then, an arm appeared out of nowhere, blocked the punch, and countered with a hit to the midsection. The gorilla slumped over, only to receive a knee to the head. Like a bag of sand, he hit the deck.

I turned. Standing before me was this tall, bodybuilding looking, blond guy. With a big toothy smile, he said, "You okay, kid?"

"Ah, yeah, thanks."

"We'd better get out of here before the cops come."

"I gotta get my friends," I pointed to them.

In a flash, he went over and cold-cocked a couple of guys. I heard a whistle and suddenly there were cops at front door. About 5 feet behind me was the back door. Miraculously, the five of us got out the back door and disappeared in seconds.

It was a good thing that we left our car so far from the grill. We jumped in and took off.

We introduced ourselves to the stranger and thanked him for the help. We were all impressed. I asked his name. He said, "Willie, but they call me Whip."

We drove him to his car. He had a beautiful white and blue Oldsmobile convertible.

"We're going down to the Lark Tavern for a pizza. You want to join us?" I asked.

"Sure. Why don't you ride with me? I'm not from around here."

I got into Willie's car and we drove to the tavern. We got to the Lark, ordered a pitcher from the bar, and got a table in the back room.

Willie told us that he was originally from Texas but moved to New York City about five years before to become a model. He was in Albany visiting his aunt for a couple of weeks.

"Oh, yeah, what kind of model?" Louie asked.

"Mostly bathing suits."

"I bet you get to meet lots of broads," Clods said, acting like a little kid.

"Not only do I meet them, but when we're on a job they dress right in front of you. I see more tits and ass than a toilet seat."

"Wow, can you introduce us?"

As I think back, our naiveté was remarkable. Here was a movie-star-looking guy, who could fight like a pro, and who appeared out of nowhere to help strangers and was a bathing suit model. We thought he was a hero. That mystery, however, was cleared up quickly.

After we finished the pizzas, Willie offered to drive Louie and me home. We put the top down, turned up the radio, and drove home with the warm summer breezes blowing on our faces, and Chuck Berry playing on the radio. He dropped Louie off first, and then he pulled up in front of my house. We talked a bit about New York and I thanked him for his rescue. My hand was still aching.

"Well, thanks again, Willie. I gotta get going."

Willie reached over and put his hand on my knee.

"You ever get your rocks off?"

"Rocks off?" The famous question with a question.

"You know, a BJ."

Oh my god, Willie was a fag, I thought.

"No, man, I don't do that. Look, my hand is killing me. I got to go soak it." I opened the door and slid out of the car, pushing his hand off my leg.

"Okay, I get it. Hey, you're not mad, are you?" Willie smiled, looking creepier by the minute.

"Na, forget about it," I said, turning and running up the front steps.

That night, I couldn't get it out of my mind. *Whip Willie was a fag. What a disappointment.*

The next day I couldn't wait to tell everyone. Nobody could believe it. Willie, the duker of dukers, was a *finocchio*!

A few days later, I was coming home from the market when I heard a horn. It was Willie.

"Hey, man, I got a six-pack. You wanna go to the drive-in?"

The drive-in, just were I wanted to go with a muscle-bound fag, I thought.

"Gee, Willie, I can't, I'm supposed to help out my Uncle Tony."

"Maybe tomorrow?"

"Maybe, I gotta go."

Willie cruised the neighborhood for the next week. I was paranoid. I left the house through the back door. I looked both ways as I walked down the street. When we were hanging out at Barbaro's, and we'd see him cruising down the street, I'd run and hide in the alley. The heat that I took from the guys was unbearable.

"Hey, here comes Willie's boy."

"Up yours," was my reply.

Willie disappeared and was never seen again.

There weren't many stories about fags in the neighborhood, princi-pally because they weren't around, and no one really looked for them. There was one gay bar in town called Clancy's. I had heard stories about guys going down there and rolling the gays for money. The most famous story involved "Crazy Richie" Gatto. He was a skinny kid who decided to buff up. Richie worked out daily and really got big. He was so taken with himself that he'd walk down the street looking at himself. He was a complete narcissist.

Richie decided that he was so good looking that he could make easy money by hustling the fags at Clancy's. As the story goes, Richie picked up this guy and instead of beating him up and getting his money, the fag beat up Richie and as a parting gift, gave him two big hickies on his neck.

Richie wore turtleneck sweaters every day during the summer's heat wave.

18

Crazy, But It Was a Living

I had so many crazy jobs I thought it best to deal with them in the next few chapters. After the organ fiasco, one would think I would have learned my lesson. However, when my lazy gene was combined with the anxiety created by being broke most of the time, the result was inevitably a crazy job.

Uncle Jack was one of the greatest salesmen of all time. Prematurely gray, big white smile, and oozing charm, Jack could sell anything. After working for the Family Record Plan, a company that sold a photograph program aimed at families with new babies, Jack went out on his own with the same product. I think he called it the International Record Association. The deal went like this.

Jack would go to the local photographers and get them to give a book of free 8x10 color portraits, each photo valued at $25. The idea was to bring people into the studio. It was a great deal for the photographers who were always trying to attract new business. Rarely would a couple leave with just one photograph, especially one of their darling new baby. They bought copies for the grandparents, uncles, aunts, and made birthday and Christmas cards with it. The photographers loved it even though Uncle Jack charged a participation fee to defray the cost of printing the coupon.

Next, to preserve the memory, he bought genuine, leather-looking photo albums for about $3 apiece. That was the product. Ten portraits valued at $250, album valued at $50, all for only $39.95—a savings of over $260. He had blue contracts for boy babies and pink for the girls. In addition, there was a gold leaf stencil with which the name of the baby could be written on the album cover. Total cost of goods sold: only $10.

The leads came from announcements in the newspaper and from public records. This was a classic, door-to-door, cold call sales deal.

Uncle Jack

Door-to-door sales are rare today because people are worried about safety and because door—to-door developed such a bad reputation over the years. In perspective, this was forty years ago. There was no Internet, no fax machines, no cable TV, or no infomercials. How else could an entrepreneur get to his customers? In addition, people were more trusting and less fearful for their safety. As result, the door was always ringing for magazines, encyclopedias, and all kinds of home improvements. And of course, there were the religion peddlers like the Jehovah's Witnesses, Seventh Day Adventists, and the Bible salesmen.

I didn't have a car so I drove my dad to work in the morning and picked him up at night. He worked for the State of New York and didn't need the car during the day. It was still another indication of how much he trusted me and of his generosity. My deal with Uncle Jack was that I made $20 on every program that I sold.

After a week of training, I was on my own. With leads in hand, I just rang the doorbells. A typical call went like this.

"Good morning, Mrs. Robinson, my name is Charles. I have a gift and an advertising presentation for your new baby. May I come in and show you?"

"Well, what is it?"

"You have been chosen as part of a national marketing survey on new baby photography to receive a gift valued at over $300."

"Well, I don't know."

"That's fine, Mrs. Robinson. I have been specifically instructed only to *offer* this gift to *you* and not to *pressure you* in any way. If you wish, I'll record that you have refused to participate, and I will offer your gift to another young mother."

"Well, no, what is the gift? Okay, come in, but I can't promise anything."

You will notice how very official everything sounded. We would typically sit in the living room. If she had other children there would be toys all over and the kids making noise. If not, the new baby might start crying. It was a real challenge to get anyone to focus.

"Congratulations on your new baby boy! What is his name?"

"Henry," she said proudly

"After the king, I assume."

"No, my father."

"Well. I can see how busy you are so I'll be brief. The National Association of Portrait Photographers (a made-up organization) is committed to preserving the fine art of portrait photography. They have joined together for this wonderful offer. Were you planning on taking any pictures of Henry?"

"Yes, of course."

"I'm sure the proud grandparents would also like to show off their new grandson."

Pulling out a coupon book from my case, "Here, we are offering not one, not two, but ten 8x10 color portraits absolutely free! With each coupon, you will receive an 8x10 color portrait valued at $25. It is just like cash, except you can't go out and buy a new hat with one. Here is a list of the fine photographers in the area who are participating. Do you recognize any of their names?"

"Oh yes, I do. I can't believe that it's free. No strings attached."

"It is free, but I can see you are a good business woman. There is one requirement. All we ask is that you preserve the portraits in this beautiful album, which is personalized with Henry's name."

"How much does that cost?"

"This album sells for over $50, but we're giving it to you at our cost of only $39.95 or only $5 per week for ten weeks. Imagine $250 in free photography for a beautiful, genuine leather-looking album at wholesale. Sounds too good to be true, doesn't it?"

"Well, I should ask my husband."

"Why ask? Wouldn't it be a great Father's Day or birthday surprise? Imagine a color portrait of his new son."

"Well, I…"

"Does your husband give you $5 a week in mad money?"

"Oh, of course, much more…Well, I guess it's okay."

I pulled out the blue contract for boys.

"Would you like your album with or without the gold lettering?"

I took out my stencil and rubbed on the name.

"Do you want to pay in full and save $10 or pay on the installment plan? We have printed these self-addressed payment envelops for your convenience."

I collected either the full amount or a $10 deposit. (Just in case she backed out, we made six bucks on the crummy album.)

I made about $500 in almost a month, and I got along famously with my uncle.

Looking back, it is hard to believe that people were so trusting. I was also surprised at how some women dressed when answering the door. One young mother answered in only a robe. As I sat on the floor making my presentation, she made sure that my view was unobstructed.

I was too chicken, and thank God I was, to do anything.

19

The Sub Mission

My father's trust at loaning his car ended with The Sub Mission. I was sitting in Walt's Sub Shop one evening, and I noticed how many college kids were buying sub sandwiches. I thought that it might be a good idea to buy the subs and sell them in the dorms.

After I haggled with Walt for a couple of days, he agreed to sell me fifty Italian Subs for 50 cents each or $25. I picked a Monday night because I thought most of the kids would be resting from the weekend. I arrived at Walt's about eight in the evening. I borrowed an apron and a picnic-looking basket from home. Walt had the subs made and piled in the corner. I paid him and loaded the subs in the trunk of the car.

It was about nine in the evening as I arrived at the State campus. I filled up my basket, put on my apron, and headed into the dorm. I took the stairs to the third floor and started knocking on doors.

"Fresh Italian subs, fresh Italian subs only a buck and half."

I was greeted with open arms. I sold ten subs on the third floor in no time. I ran down to the car and filled up the basket again. As I walked in a second time, the dorm director met me—a big, tall officious guy, with his hands on his hips. He looked like a can of Raid.

"Can I help you?" he said in a condescending way.

"Fresh, delicious Italian subs from Walt's. Here, have one on me."

"Do you have authorization?"

"From Walt?"

"No, from food service."

"Why?"

"You can't sell food in the dorms without authorization. And since the cafeteria sells subs, I doubt you'll get it."

"Yeah, but I heard the ones they sell suck," I was trying to be funny.

"Get out before I call the campus police."

I walked out discouraged, but not defeated. I tried another dorm and was caught again. Finally, I stood in the middle of the dorm quadrangle and yelled, "Fresh Italian subs, fresh Italian subs, only a buck and half."

This time the campus police escorted my car off campus. I had sold about twenty subs. It was about eleven and I was tired. I only lost $5. *Could have been worse,* I thought. When I got home, I ate a couple of subs and went to bed. I could eat like that in those days and sleep like a baby.

My father took the next day off to do some work in the yard. It was one of those hot September days. I slept late, and about noon, my father shook me awake

"Get up, get up."

"What the matter?"

"Get up!" he said, as angry as I have ever seen him.

Still in my pajamas, I was grabbed and escorted outside. He opened the car door, sat me in the front seat, and closed the door. The smell was overwhelming. With the sun baking on the car, it must have been 140 degrees in the trunk. My forgotten subs were ripening in the trunk.

"I need to take your mother out tonight. Any suggestions?"

"Dad, I'm really sorry. I totally forgot. I was going to get rid of them, but I overslept."

"What are you going to do with them?"

"I'll take them to the dump."

"Here's a better idea, you take them to Pa's and bury them in the tomato garden. They'll make great fertilizer."

It was work, but that was my punishment. I buried the subs in the garden, washed out the trunk, and sprayed it with Lysol. The smell went away in a few days.

My car borrowing days were over, but the tomato crop the next spring was spectacular!

20

The Boring Bank Gives Birth to Eulato

The National Commercial Bank and Trust Company was the biggest bank in town. My mother worked in the executive cafeteria at lunchtime. She found out from one of the execs that the Loan Department was hiring students to work from five to nine in the evening calling customers who were late on their installment loans. I applied and got hired. The HR person loved my mother.

The bank hired six of us on an experimental basis. We reported to the bank as the bank closed in the evening. One of the bank's managers was assigned each evening to supervise the group. Given today's technology, it is hard to imagine how such a primitive program existed. These installment loans were for cars, boats, and home improvements for which the bank recorded payments on 6x9 cards. The cards were kept in long trays.

Each card carried the name on the account, address, phone number, account number, amount of loan, monthly due date, monthly payment amount, payment history, and delinquent charges. After about ten minutes of training on how to read the card, we were put to work.

After we arrived with our coffee and snacks, followed by a few minutes of socializing, we lined up at a vault entrance and were handed a tray. Each tray held approximately one thousand cards. Our job was to thumb through the cards until we reached a late or missing payment.

We then would call the account and prompt them to pay. We gave ourselves AKAs to protect our identities. After all, no one wanted to be known as an evil collector. Dick was Robert Roy, Gordon was Buddy Frank, Artie was Sheldon Keats, and I was Michael Hunt.

Dinnertime was the best time to call. Here's a typical call:

"Hello, Mrs. Hannity, this is Mike Hunt (sorry, I couldn't help myself) from the National Commercial Bank. How are you this evening?"

"Fine, thank you."

"I am calling about your August payment on your 1959 Pontiac. I have noticed that you have been late four out of the last six months. Is there anything wrong?"

"My husband has been sick and…" she pleaded.

"Oh, I'm sorry to hear that, but you are paying money for late charges that could be used for medicine."

"Oh, I know but it's been very hard."

"And we're trying to be understanding, Mrs. Hannity. The last thing we ever want to happen is for you to have to take a cab to the doctor's office."

As you can see, this was not a pleasant job. Some of the calls were hilarious while others were incredibly sad. Unfortunately, we were there to collect money and not to be sympathetic. After the first week, we all became calloused to people's misfortunes. Even if we were sympathetic, we couldn't help other than waive a late payment. On the other hand, it is remarkable how creative some people can be about not paying their bills.

The job was depressing, but the money was pretty good. On our breaks we discussed ways of meeting girls and making money. Dick Euler and I came up with the idea of running dances so local college kids could mix. That way, we thought, we could solve both problems.

There were half a dozen colleges in the area. It should be a snap to draw a few hundred people to a mixer.

We formed EULATO Enterprises, a combination of our names. The Ten Eyck Hotel was a grand old property located about two blocks from the bank that had a huge ballroom perfect for our needs.

The next day we made an appointment with the food and beverage director of the hotel about an hour before work. Mr. Byrnes was a nice guy. We presented him with the following deal. He would give us the ballroom. We'd provide the band and the people. We'd take the gate, and the hotel took the bar—simple, clean, and brilliant.

Since the hotel was virtually empty most Friday nights, he liked the idea and agreed to give it a try. We shook hands, and Eulato was out of the gate, or out **for** the gate, as it were.

We had four weeks to pull this off. We did most of the work on the bank's time. We printed posters and cards proclaiming the following:

"The Intercollegiate Mixer"

The only event ever to bring together all

The Tri-cities Colleges and Universities.

The biggest event of the year!

Limited space, get there early

Food and refreshments

Brought to you

By

The Intercollegiate Coalition & Eulato Enterprises—first in fun

Admission $2.00

We listed the school, fraternity, and sorority names on the poster. Jackets for men recommended—in those days college kids dressed.

We drove around town and put up posters everywhere: on telephone poles, in cafeterias, on bulletin boards, and in the dorms The Intercollegiate Coalition existed only in our imagination. We made it up to sound official. It worked. No one challenged us and our posters went everywhere. Boy, did we have balls.

Since it was a hotel, we had to hire the band through the union. We found a six-piece rock group who agreed to play for $125 for four hours.

We were so unsophisticated that it was pathetic. We bought a roll of tickets and a stamp with a big "I" and a stamp pad. We set up about seven. The band was to play from eight to twelve. We had a folding table and a tablecloth set at the ballroom entrance, and signs placed all over the hotel. The hotel provided the cash bar and put out some chips.

We had no idea whether this would work. By 7:30 two nerds showed up. We started to panic. Finally, as if the floodgates opened, people suddenly started pouring into the hotel. We couldn't collect the money fast enough. By nine o'clock, over 500 showed and we collected over $1000. The place was rocking.

We were geniuses. After expenses, we netted almost $700. It was big money for a couple of seventeen-year-olds.

We ran one more with moderate success, then disaster hit. We unknowingly scheduled a mixer on one of the busiest nights of the year.

We didn't check the calendars thoroughly enough. There were home-comings, reunions, football games. It was very stupid of us.

On disaster night, as we fondly named it, we attracted only fifty women and ten guys. The ratio was great for the guys, but the numbers were pathetic. The girls kept asking when were the guys coming. We told them that that the bus broke down. Dick and I knew we were in trouble. I paid the band. Since we only collected $120, I took $5 out of my own pocket. We grabbed our metal box and sneaked out the back stairs. With printing, etc., we lost about $300.

Bad news grows as it travels. The Intercollegiate Mixer was history, as was Eulato Enterprises—the company who for an instant was known as *first in fun*.

21

Always Friendly, Never Familiar

Christmastime of my senior year was when I was out looking for work again. A mysterious store was located across the park from the state capitol building. It was a classic, three-story brick building that sold men's clothing on one side of the building, and women's on the other. It was mysterious to me because I never saw anyone ever go in or come out of the store.

I asked around and found that W. E. Walsh and Sons was a super exclusive clothing store that catered to the legislators and the city's upper class. I peeked in the window. The store looked like a club, with oak-paneled walls and thick carpeting on the staircase. The salesmen looked like valets ready to dress the Lord of the Manor. It was intimidating, but intriguing.

I went home, shined up my cordovans, pressed my pants, brushed my maroon and black sport coat, and, first thing the next day, I headed back downtown and walked into the store. The salesman approached.

"How may I help you?" he asked smugly.

"Ah yeah, are you hiring any extra help for Christmas?"

"Extra help? Christmas?" There was an awkward pause.

He turned toward the other salesman.

"Charles, are we hiring any…extra help…for Christmas, that is?"

"I don't know. Ask Mr. Crummy."

Mr. Crummy was the son-in-law of the owner and the store manager. He had an airy, proper quality.

Just then, Mr. Crummy came floating down the staircase.

"Are we hiring for Christmas?" Charles inquired.

Crummy looked me up and down.

"I'll check with Mr. Walsh." He walked into Mr. Walsh's office.

Mr. Walsh had his office behind the shirt counter. A hidden door that looked like it led into a closet actually opened into a small office. Mr. Walsh had a roll-top desk and a ceiling fan. No one ever entered this space uninvited except for Crummy.

The door opened, a hand stretched out and motioned me in.

I walked into this secret room and saw a distinguished elderly gentleman. He was lean, had flowing white hair, and was dressed in a beautifully tailored charcoal pinstripe suit, white starched shirt, and maroon paisley tie.

"I am Bill Walsh and this is the store manager, Ed Crummy," he said in a very friendly way. "We have never hired any *part-time* help. What brings you into the store?"

"I was passing by and it looked like a nice place," I said.

"Honest answer, I like that. Do you have any experience working in haberdashery?"

I had no idea what that meant. I never heard the word before. Winging it, I said, "No, but I've been wearing haberdashery since I can remember."

The two of them started laughing. They thought that was the funniest thing.

"Are you in school? How old are you?"

"Seventeen. I am a senior at CBA."

"Good school. I went to Albany Military Academy many years ago. What's your rank?"

"Cadet Captain, sir."

"Very impressive! Do you own anything more…subdued?" Referring to my sport jacket.

"No, sir." I liked this guy.

"Well, Mr. Crummy, maybe we can fix that. We are open every night until nine until Christmas. Can you get here by four?"

"Yes, sir, and school is out for two weeks so I can work longer if you need me."

"We'll deal with that later. For now, you are on probation. If your work is satisfactory, you will be extended."

"Thank you, sir." I turned to leave.

"Do you expect to be paid?"

"Oh yes, I forgot…"

Whispering to Crummy, then pausing. "How does $1.75 per hour sound, plus a discount on whatever you buy?"

"Okay, when do I start?"

"Mr. Crummy will check your references and take care of the details."

He shook my hand and dismissed me. Crummy led me up the stairs to the women's level where he introduced me to the ladies, then to his office where I filled out some paperwork for taxes and references, and then up the back stairs to the shipping department where I was given a locker. The shipping guy, Oscar, doubled as a furrier—an interesting combination, I thought. As it turned out, Oscar and I became good friends. I would go up and bullshit with him during my breaks. He gave me all the gossip on a store that had been around since the turn of the century and on the people, some of whom looked as though they had been around almost as long. He also showed me how pelts were cut and fitted to make fur coats.

I reported the next day, and they replaced my maroon and black hounds tooth with a tasteful, gray blazer. As I reflect, it was like a finishing school.

I was shown how to walk, stand, and, most importantly, how to make the rich feel comfortable. The lessons were memorable. Mr. Crummy showed me the ropes. I can still hear his articulate, denasalized voice.

> Always walk slowly toward the customer so as to not startle him. Slightly tip your head and pleasantly ask if you can be of any help. If not, step back, hands comfortably behind your back, and stand quietly and wait to be summoned. When not busy, make sure that the shelves are properly stocked, and that the merchandise is neatly and tastefully presented. If you know the customer's name, always address him or her as Mr. or Mrs. Remember, **always friendly, never familiar**.
>
> We sell only the finest product. Oxford with five-point tailoring is the top of the line priced from $300. Next is Hickey Freeman, also a superior garment, priced from $175. For the younger, more athletic figure, we carry H. Freeman, priced for the junior executive from $125. The Troy Shirt Makers Guild makes our shirts from the finest cottons and silks. A. Sulka provides our silk ties and cotton and silk underwear.

They went on to show me how to guess sizes and how to measure for shirts and suits.

> To measure for a shirt: For the neck size, place the tape loosely on the neck just below the Adam's apple. For the sleeve, raise the arm so that it is parallel to the floor bent at the elbow. Place the tape at the center of the back at the base of the collar and measure to the elbow. Holding the tape at the elbow, continue around to the bump on the wrist.

If the gentleman is interested in a suit, escort him to the suit department on the mezzanine. Help him remove his jacket, if he's wearing one. Find out his color and fabric preferences. Look at him carefully and suggest a size. If he looks like a 46 long suggest a 44 long. If you are going to error, error in flattering way. Select a 46 off the rack, if it fits only mention your mistake after he removes it. For example, *"Oh, this is a 46, I grabbed it in error. How did it feel?"* We carry sizes from 36 to 50. They come in short, extra short, regular, long and extra long. If a gentlemen is large around the middle, you might want to suggest a portly, never fat, never husky always portly. The difference between the jacket size and waist is called the drop. The normal drop is 5 inches to 6 inches. For example, a 42 jacket comes with a 36- to 37-inch waist on the pants. An athletic drop is eight inches. In this case, a 42 would have a 34 waist.

After all this training, I was still required to shadow the salesmen until they were convinced that I knew what I was doing and wouldn't embarrass the store. Within a week or two I was on my own. I assume I was doing it right because they allowed me to work full time during my vacation. It was a great job. The people were all nice. It added an additional dimension to my outlook on life. I got my first view of how successful people think and work. I worked at the store every year until I graduated from college. They were very generous in allowing me to buy clothes at their cost—allowing me to look as well as act the part.

22

Some Senior Moments

My senior year at CBA began with my receiving a commission as Cadet Captain making my mother very proud. I had earned enough money to buy new uniforms so finally everything was custom-fitted. I now carried a sword and, when in full dress, a sash, tar bucket, and plume, plus stars on my collar indicating "Wadesboro rifles," reflecting academic performance. In August, we oriented the freshman. I thought I'd enjoy harassing the guys but I was more interested in teaching them. I guess that maturity may have been sneaking up on me.

Captain Coose

I was originally assigned to the band company, but then was transferred to G Company as company commander. Colonel Smith, who was the PMS&T assigned by the army, liked me. I think he sensed that

I was a street kid, and he always went out of his way to be helpful. I recognized it, I appreciated it, and I think he knew it.

He called me into his office and told me that G Company was a problem. For some reason, all the "screw-ups" in the school were assigned to this company. The school would deny it, but I think it was because G was last in line during drill and the Company wouldn't be noticed as much. Also, by putting them together, they hopefully would be easier to control. These were well-to-do, spoiled kids who were at military school under duress. The colonel told me that he had faith in me, and to come to him if there were any problems.

It was easy to spot the "screw-ups." They were generally upperclassmen with no rank, shaggy hair, wrinkled uniforms. It was so easy to acquire rank. The major components required were passing the easy military tests and daily inspection. To pass the inspections only required wearing shined shoes and pressed pants and shirt. If you passed only half the tests and inspections, you got your corporal or sergeant stripes. To reach the senior year as a private was to be a successful failure, i.e., one had to strive for failure and succeed.

My first drill as G Company commander was a hoot. The company looked like a mob. With every upper-class private in the regiment and my officers being the regiment's party guys, it definitely was a challenge. Since it became clear that discipline was impossible, damage control was my only salvation.

I pulled the seniors aside and made a deal. I would not hassle anyone, but in exchange, all I asked was for them to do their best, i.e., just look good when someone was watching. I let them smoke, talk while drilling, and was liberal with inspections. Remember that every demerit required twenty-five minutes of marching around the flagpole after school.

We had a secret code command. Whenever I shouted, "company eyes up," it meant someone was watching, and for a few minutes, we looked like a crack drill team. It was during one of those moments that I got "the idea."

Once a year in the spring the regiment put on a Formal Drill Night for the parents, JROTC officials, and alumni. It was held in the evening at the Washington Avenue Armory. It was the regiment's show of the year.

I made an appointment to meet with Colonel Smith and presented an idea that would create a way to get seniors motivated and entertain the guests at the annual drill event. Colonel Smith thought for moment, laughed, and said, "Go ahead, it sounds like fun." But, he warned me, "If it's not done in a disciplined way, you'll look like an idiot."

At the next drill, I presented the idea to the company. The seven senior privates would put on a show that would be their last chance to poke fun at real buttoned-up cadets.

Instead of a crack precision drill team, we would present the "cracked drill team." I explained that it would be hard work, and every move had to be choreographed. Everything scripted, even the ad-libs. Where the real precision team did everything right, our cracked team would do everything wrong.

Just because they were the screw-ups didn't mean that they were dumb. Actually, they all had above-average intelligence, and this idea really bonded them. They took hold of the idea and for the first time that I had seen, they really worked hard. They loved the idea that it was all to be kept a strict secret.

For the next four drills, we drilled an hour with the regiment and then G Company disappeared.

Annual Drill Night for G Company was like opening night on Broadway. I never saw the guys more excited. No one in the entire school, including the Brothers, knew what was about to happen.

The program began with the regiment marching onto the floor to the sounds of John Phillips Sousa. The reviewing stands were packed with family, alumni, and officials. The regiment then presented the colors and played the national anthem. Next, the regiment marched around for pass-in-review. The JROTC appointment was presented, followed by speeches and awards. The regiment then stood at parade rest in formation on the far side of the floor opposite the reviewing stand.

The precision drill team then awed the crowd with their crisp, close order moves and fancy rifle salutes.

Following the applause I shouted, "G Companeeeey, for-ward...march."

G Company marched onto the center floor and positioned itself in front of the reviewing stand. Everyone looked baffled. This wasn't on the printed program.

"Company, halt," I ordered. "Right...face! Parade...rest! Lt. Robinson, front and center!"

Robinson broke from the ranks, positioned himself in front of me, "Lt. Robinson reporting, sir!"

"Lt. Robinson, are you aware that your platoon is missing a squad?" I said.

"Missing a squad, sir?" He replied.

"Maybe you should check." Robinson turned smartly, inspected his platoon, and did an about-face.

"You are correct, sir."

"May I ask where they are?"

"I think they went for a drink, sir."

"Went for a drink. Did you forget this is our annual review? What kind of drink?"

"Not sure, sir. They might be lost!"

"Lost! How could..."

Just then, from the back room of the Amory came the lost squad. Led by Corporal Pimento, the squad marched to the center of the floor between G Company and the reviewing stand. Pimento was one of the larger cadets in the regiment. At 5 feet 8, he was as wide as he was tall.

Hats on crooked, uniforms unbuttoned, one of the Cadets dragging his rifle on the floor, the squad looked like they were recovering from a ghastly hangover.

"Squad...halt," Pimento commanded, turned and saluted.

"Corporal Pimento, where have you been?"

"Practicing, sir."

"Practicing what?"

"Practicing our close-order drill, sir."

"Well, that's impressive. Show me what you've learned."

"Yes, sir!" He saluted and did an about-face.

"Left...face."

They turned left *almost* together.

"Right shoulder...arms! Left shoulder...arms!"

Again performed *almost* together.

"Present...arms."

On command, they all threw their rifles at Pimento. (We gave them fake wooden guns.) The audience finally got the gag and the laughter broke out.

With the precision of an Abbot and Costello routine, they kept the audience in stitches for the next ten minutes. They ended the show with a surprise. The Queen Anne's Salute is a precision move that is included in every drill show. Instead of bungling the salute, they performed the salute perfectly. They marched back to the company and with total precision rejoined the platoon. I marched G Company off the floor to a standing ovation. It was incredibly gratifying to see how proud my company of misfits was of their performance.

I had continued my interest in the theater since the "Passion Play" introduction two years earlier. During my senior year, the school decided to do Reginald Rose's *Twelve Angry Men,* the story of a jury deliberating a murder case. You may have seen the movie with Henry Fonda and Lee J. Cobb. I played juror number eight, the part Henry Fonda made famous.

We built a platform in the middle of the gym and performed the play in the round. The play was a success and the reviews in the newspaper were pretty good. The play helped me choose to be a theater major when I later started at the State University of New York at Albany.

Just when I thought that I had matured and was full of self-confidence, the Aunt "Mary Mustacchi" incident occurred.

Each day after school I walked home. It was about two miles. One Thursday, after our weekly drill, I was headed down Holland Avenue with three members of my company. I was wearing my dress blues, complete with sword, sash, tar bucket, and plume.

Next to Holland was a large open field. It consisted of several undeveloped acres and was owned by the city. Since it wasn't being used, the city would issue permits for people to plant and grow small gardens. My Aunt "Mary Mustacchi"—since we had so many Marys in the family, we always added the husband's name for identification—who was from an agricultural family in southern Italy, was issued one of those permits.

In her garden she grew tomatoes, squash, fennel, cabbage, and other vegetables. This was an ambitious task. My Uncle Mustacchi, her husband, retired from the railroad. He hurt his leg falling from the train. He went on permanent disability and received a small monthly check. He stayed home and sat on the front porch where he acted like a big shot philosopher and gave out dimes like John D. Rockefeller.

Mary, who was less than 5 feet tall and weighed less than a hundred pounds, worked at the linen laundry all day, washing, carrying large bundles, and ironing in oppressive heat. After work, she tended her garden. In her remaining spare time, she cooked and cleaned for her husband. She had snow-white hair that she tied in a ball in the back of her head. She only wore black dresses and had a voice that was pitched high enough to break glass. At harvest time she put the vegetables in a baby carriage and pushed the carriage home where she distributed the produce to family and friends.

As I was coming down the hill, she was headed for the street from the field. With eyes as sharp as an eagle, she spotted me.

"Carlucci," she yelled like a siren cutting through the quiet breeze.

My heart sank, *Oh no*, I thought. Acting like I didn't hear, I kept walking.

"Carlucci," she yelled again. This time one of my friends tugged on my sleeve.

"There's a tiny old lady in a black dress pushing a baby carriage who is trying to get your attention."

I stopped, took a deep breath. "Wait a second, guys, it's my aunt." I suddenly realized that I hadn't gotten over my insecurities. I had carefully kept my two worlds separated. Now they were about to collide. The blood was already rushing to my face. We stood there as this 4-foot-10-inch person pushing a giant baby carriage filled with vegetables, approached us.

"Hey, Carlucci, howa come youa don't stop for a youra Aunt Mary? Whata, are you ashamed?"

"No. Aunt Mary. I didn't hear you."

"Coma ovea here, and givea youra Aunta Mary a kiss!"

Shit, I thought, *here we go with the kissing again.* "I can't. I'm not allowed to kiss anyone when I'm in uniform."

"You kissa your Aunt Mary or I givea you a baciaroni (slap in the face)." My face was getting more flushed.

I bent over so far that my tar bucket fell off my head and landed in the carriage. I gave her a kiss.

"That'sa better. Howsa you mother?"

"Great."

"Howsa you father?"

"Great."

"Here, I gotta something for them."

She reached in the carriage and pulled out a squash as big as small tuba.

"Here, givea this *cugootz* to your mama."

"You want me to carry *that* home?"

"Wa sure."

"I can't. I'm in uniform. Why don't you mail it?"

"You taka this a home or I…!" She said angrily biting her index finger.

"Okay, okay!"

I tucked the squash under my arm and started home. It was the longest trip of my life. My friends didn't say a word. I kept thinking how stupid I must have looked carrying a ten-pound squash under my arm. When I got home, I told my mother how Aunt Mary embarrassed me. I don't know now why it was so traumatic. I ranted and raved for hours. When you are eighteen, no matter how cool you think you are, you are still an insecure kid.

On the positive side, that little scene did prepare me for my graduation. Graduation ceremonies were filled with pomp and ceremony. We wore dress white uniforms. The entire regiment attended and conducted a full drill program. There were guest speakers and awards.

In the midst of all these formalities stood my family ready to celebrate. They all showed: my parents, my grandparents, my aunts, and my uncles. As the crowd politely applauded the pass and review, my family danced, cheered, whistled, and pointed.

As I marched past them, I couldn't help but smile. It isn't exactly Mrs. Potter's finishing school, but they're all mine!

23

Glad to Grad

Graduation Day was a unique experience. I awoke in the morning with a whirlwind of emotions bumping around my head. First there was relief. I learned what I was required to learn, and proved it by passing the test. In New York State in those days, they had State exams called the Regents. They were taken in all the major subjects and were designed to ensure a certain proficiency. We bought these study guides published by Barron's that showed the type of questions and how to answer them.

After relief comes sadness. You are leaving something that grew familiar and dominated your consciousness for the past four years. The new friends were now old friends, and with few exceptions, it was unlikely that there would be much future contact. The school chapter had a beginning, middle, and end, and it was now time to move on.

After sadness came fear. I was eighteen and on the cusp of adulthood, at least in this country. In other cultures, where the young are less coddled, I'd be middle-aged with a family. Still, there was the fear of the unknown. There had been unknowns before, but for some reason, this seemed more serious and more challenging.

Finally, there came excitement and anticipation. I was aware of my changes in the past and was excited about how I would change in the future. There would be new faces, new places, and hopefully a better understanding of how to best work the world. I sensed, but couldn't articulate at the time, that if I didn't learn to work the world, the world would work me.

G Company

But today was for celebration. Graduation parade and ceremonies started at noon. As the company commander of the party company, it wasn't a surprise that we planned a pre-graduation get-together. Lt. Robinson had arranged for a keg in his garage. Drinking to commence at 10 AM. I packed my dress whites in anticipation of Pimento picking me up at about 9:30 AM. Before leaving, I begged my mother to keep the family group small and to give them strict instructions to behave. She promised and then started crying over how proud she was of me. She gave me a big hug.

"After graduation we're having a party for you. All your cousins, aunts, and uncles have been invited," she said, looking for my excitement.

"Great!" I said

"We'll have lots of food and drink. Why don't you invite a few of your friends over?"

"Ma, you're not serious, are you?"

"Why?" she asked innocently.

"Ma, look around, we live in a flat, on the second floor, on Second Avenue. My friends have houses with big yards, with party tents, on streets with dreamy names. Why would anyone come down here?"

She looked sad. I think I hurt her feelings.

"Look, Ma, I love you and I love this house. I'm sorry, I hurt your feelings but…Okay, I'll mention it to a few of the guys." I kissed her and left.

Robinson's garage was jumping. There were about a dozen guys and girls, hot dogs on the grill, and a big keg of Dobler Beer in the corner. Drinking age was eighteen so we were all legal.

We were having such a good time we almost forgot about graduation. I had a couple of beers and hot dogs. I felt a little high but was okay. Conversely, half of my company had slightly overindulged. Well, maybe slightly was an understatement.

We piled into half a dozen cars and headed merrily to the school. Formation was set up in the parking lot behind the armory. It must have been about 95 degrees and humid—perfect conditions for digesting hot dogs and beer.

We finished dressing and tried to look presentable. Just as the marching beat of the drums announced the appearance of the regiment, the barfing began. As usual, it was unfortunately contagious. It sounded like a foghorn convention.

As the last company in the order of the regiment, it took about five minutes before we started to move. It was a good thing because it gave us time to regroup. It was a necessary thing because we needed to get away from the smell of the barf.

I pleaded with the company to get their shit together.

"This is our last time. Our families are out there. Please don't pass out."

As we started to move out, the barfing seemed to have ended. The band played "Stars and Stripes Forever" as we passed the reviewing stand. Everything seemed fine until we lined up for presenting of the colors. The command was "Present...arms." For the officers it meant drawing the sword and bringing the handle to the lips with the blade facing upward at a 45-degree angle.

As soon as "arms" left my lips, I heard "Heads up, Captain." I looked up only to see a sword floating in the air arching down to where I was standing. I took a step back just as the sword plunged to the ground landing about two feet in front on me. It stuck in the grass and vibrated like a tuning fork. I turned to the company. Lt. Robinson had his hand frozen to his lips as if he were still holding the sword.

"It slipped," he said with a guilty, apologetic look. The whole company was shaking with silent laughter.

"As you were," I commanded. "Retrieve sword...March!"

Robinson marched to his sword, pulled it from the ground as if it were part of the drill.

It was a miracle that I didn't get skewered. I think God was telling me that the military was not in my future. I looked up and whispered, "Thanks, God, I get the point."

A bigger miracle was that no one noticed that G Company was wasted. We received our diplomas, tossed our hats in celebration, and joined our families. We took a couple of pictures with the family and left. I mentioned to my mother that I had invited a couple of guys over but I doubted anyone would show.

We arrived home just after four. I got out of my uniform and helped set up for the party. We set up a big buffet in the dining room with Italian cold cuts, a turkey, ham and roasts, cheeses, cut veggies, and all kinds of salads. My relatives brought lasagna, antipasto, sausage and peppers, pizza, and yards of desserts. We filled the bathtub with ice, beer, and soda.

Around six o'clock, it started. One by one, members of my graduation class started to show up. By eight, nearly fifty out of the eighty in the graduating class were at my house. They were hanging out on both front porches, in the living room, and in the yard. Counting the girls they brought, and my relatives, the number rose to more than one hundred and fifty. My brother, who was ten at the time, was collecting tips from delivering beers. I think he made more than $25.

It was as if they had never eaten. They devoured everything. My mother was in heaven and kept on sending my cousin, Anthony, to Barbaro's for more food. My dad was playing the accordion, and people were singing and dancing.

It was nearing midnight when we realized that it was time to shut down. The food and beer were gone and still no one was leaving.

My brother-in-law, Jack, started yelling "Big Party at Slattery's house, plenty of beer," as he escorted them out the front door.

We cleared the house, grabbed a coffee, and collapsed in the living room.

I sat quietly and smiled as a tear rolled down my cheek. I thought, *I guess being a street kid only mattered to me.*

24

So, You're a College Boy

There was never a doubt that I would go to college. It was only a question of where. My only limitation was it had to cost little or nothing. My list consisted of one that met that criteria, and that was before I had eliminated any from the list. The State University of New York at Albany at the time had no tuition, and I could live at home. Since there were no uniforms to buy, it ended up cheaper than high school and a real bargain.

The year that I started it was called State Teacher's College. Good old Nelson Rockefeller, then the governor, decided that the capitol city of the Empire State needed a showcase university, one that would rival California's famous university system. Looking like something out of the twenty-first century, this multimillion-dollar project, completed in 1966, was designed with an academic podium in the center, surrounded by four residential twenty-three-story towers. Each tower was then surrounded by a residential quadrangle.

I spent most of my time at the old campus. It was made up of several traditional red brick buildings and was set in the heart of deteriorating Albany. Only a few miles from my home, it was a convenient walk on a nice day. The new campus wasn't completed until my senior year and my class was the first to graduate.

The weekend before classes started, the freshman and sophomores arrived early to conduct a tradition called "rivalry." There was food,

165

beer, dancing, and singing—all very corny, but appropriate for the time. The big thing was the competition.

We had cutsie names. The freshmen were the "Blue Jays" and the sophomores were the "Red Devils." There were races, treasure hunts, and a singing competition. We had to write a fight song and a class song. Since I was pretty good at parodies, I wrote both.

Unfortunately, we won the song competition and I was elected the class song leader for the next year. I didn't look like or act like a song leader, nor did I want to be a song leader. In other words, I wasn't a cheerleader. These "rah-rah" people were not only a new breed to me, but they made me uncomfortable.

Having spent the last four years in an all-boys' school, I definitely did like having women around. Because it was a teachers' college, the ratio of women to men was at least five to one. It was like falling into a room filled with ice cream sundaes. My poverty had helped me make an excellent educational decision.

Did I mention that getting laid was my life? As much as I hated the class song leader title, it did provide a cover for my predatory nature. I took this opportunity to meet as many women as possible. For an eighteen-year-old male, it was not about relationships, commitments, discretion, communicating, or finding a mate. It was about biological releases. Looking around at the quadrangle filled with women, all I could see were targets.

If I didn't carry the guilt of being the first one in the family to attend college and if I had had the money, I probably would have stretched my college experience out from four to eight years or maybe have been a professional student. I could already tell that academia creates a wonderfully unrealistic environment not only for the ideologue, but also for the person who finds responsibility to be a burden.

Although I was planning on being a theater major, I didn't have to declare a major until the end of my second year. I contend that the first semester in college is the most critical. Either you get the system or you don't. If you get the system, you can drink and party until your liver falls out, or until the infirmary runs out of penicillin, and still succeed.

Unfortunately, under this philosophy, learning is secondary but passing the course is paramount. My theory is if you go to *all* the classes with the objective of trying to *figure out what is important,* you'll not only learn by osmosis, but it will create a skill at setting priorities that you can use throughout your life. Sounds noble, doesn't it?

First thing needed is a selfish teacher—an intellectual snob who regards underclassmen as groundlings and who only exists as a teacher so that he can establish his credibility for writing and/or getting paid for consulting, This is an A if you suck up, a B if he just knows your name, and a C if you take the test but your handwriting for the essay is incomprehensible and your answer is long.

I was assigned an advisor from the Theater Department. He was an assistant professor or some equally low-level position. A nice enough guy, he was a little light on his feet, but sincere. We talked about courses and study habits. I lived at home, so we didn't get into dorm life. I added an acting course in addition to the usual freshman lecture hall requirements so as to "get the flavor," as Mr. Stetson phrased it, of the department.

Since I was a morning person, I scheduled all my classes before noon except for a biology lab on Wednesdays at four o'clock. There wasn't much noteworthy about my first day of class. The only thing that bothered me was the lecture hall with two hundred students. It was so impersonal and dry that I didn't know how I could stay awake. The professor definitely wanted to be somewhere else.

Acting class, on the other hand, was small and very personal. Actors, although naturally neurotic, are friendly and sensitive. They are also grubby. The early sixties was still a time for the clean-cut, all-American look, except for the bikers, beatniks, and serious artsy folk.

After class, the group invited me to the cafeteria for some coffee. The cafeteria was broken down into three rooms. There was a room for faculty, located on the opposite side of the kitchen, and then two adjoining rooms. The larger, brighter room was for the mainstream students, fraternities, and sororities. The smaller, darker room, called the "cave," was for the artsy people—theater, art majors, writers, and anarchists.

I picked up my coffee and sat down at a larger round table in the cave. Everyone was very friendly, with upperclassmen and freshmen mixing very comfortably. People talked about the shows they worked, the upcoming schedule of plays, and of course, man's inhumanity to man.

In spite of all the literary talk, the cave had a loser quality to it. It was dark and had no windows, while the general cafeteria looked clean and bright. Looking back, it reminded me of the scene in the Italian film directed by Franco Brusati, titled *Bread and Chocolate*. The immigrant workers were held up in a chicken coop watching the beautiful, semi-naked society people cavorting with their horses in the woods. This was the first sign that maybe I was in the wrong place. I even dressed differently. I wore a blue buttoned-down shirt and V-neck sweater while my table mates were in sweatshirts and khaki, army-looking safari jackets. I looked out of place yet I was getting their attention almost as if they had captured me from the other side. I began to realize that this was as much a political statement as it was literary. As I think back, I was hearing the same liberal, political social commentary that I find so irritating today. My introduction to the theater crowd was already headed in the wrong direction.

As the semester progressed, my circle of friends widened. Some of the mainstream/fraternity guys with whom I met at rivalry were evolving into friends. Now whenever I went to the cafeteria, I had to make the decision whether to go into the cave with the artsy folk, or go into the main room with the frat guys.

As much as I loved the theater, I didn't like theater people. They were too emotional, neurotic, liberal, and pretentious for my taste. The girls, surprisingly, weren't that great-looking, and were definitely more needy—a trait that even at my young age I sensed was trouble. After a few weeks, when I did sit in the cave, I was bored in ten minutes. The frat guys, on the other hand, talked about drinking, sports, and girls with just the right level of irresponsibility for my still immature, very active libido.

Another crossroad was about to be reached. I did love the excitement of the theater and the ego-boosting quality of the acting but still liked to party and raise hell. They say you can take the kid from the street, but you can't take the street from the kid.

My greatest insecurity has always been not having any money. It was the force that drove my entrepreneurial spirit. What if I couldn't make a living as an actor, what would I do? Teach? By the end of my first semester, it occurred to me that I needed a hedge.

I met with my advisor, and we discussed my dilemma. As a theater person, he talked about his love for the art form, how happy it made him just to be around it. He still did summer stock, but after several years he had decided "to give up the full-time struggle of the professional stage for the role of a pedagogue in the theatre of academia." His answer made *him* teary eyed and made *me* think of the end of a Bugs Bunny cartoon, "Well, that's All, Folks."

The music came up, and I exited stage left.

25

Fo di ro li ro ro ro!

Our freshman year we came to State
Fo di ro li ro ro ro
  We started drinking Haig and Haig
  Fo di ro li ro ro ro
Our sophomore year we came back here
Fo di ro li ro ro ro
  No more whiskey, we drank beer
  Fo di ro li ro ro ro
Our junior year we were so broke
Fo di ro li ro ro ro
  To a drinking man, this is no joke
  Fo di ro li ro ro ro
The saddest tale we have to tell
Fo di ro li ro ro ro
  Is when we bid the keg farewell
  Fo di ro li ro ro ro!

At the end of my first semester, I requested a new advisor. Mr. Wright was a professor in the Business Department where he taught a stock and finance course. He was a short, jolly guy in his fifties with a round face, thick-rimmed glasses, and a slight limp. I told him of my conflicting feelings and asked his advice. He had the attention span of a fruit fly—not exactly advisor material.

After taking a call from his stockbroker, he turned, collected his thoughts, shrugged his shoulders and said, "I just lost my ass on soybeans. You want to buy a few bushels? Just kidding. Now, where were we?"

"I was telling you about…"

"Yeah, yeah," he interrupted as he finally got focused. "I remember now. No big deal, you can do both."

"How could I do that?"

"You could be a business major and minor in theater. You'll need 36 course hours in your major and 18 in your minor. Not much when you consider you need 128 course hours to graduate. You could even do a double major."

"Sounds great, but I'm not that ambitious."

"You could be an artsy-fartsy businessman," he said, laughing at his own not-so-clever cleverness.

"Funny."

"I got it." The image of a light bulb appeared over his head. "You could also minor in Phys Ed, wear pink sneakers, and become a drama coach." He was on a roll.

"Now that was funny. What do I have to do?"

"As a business major, you'd get a Bachelors of Science rather than Arts. Take a few more math and science courses, but you don't have to take a language if you don't want to. I'll be your advisor as long as you don't bother me too much. We'll work out the schedule. It's a little late but I'll get you in."

I liked the guy. He was hysterical, and my kind of iconoclast. Even though he didn't act all that devoted, I found out as our friendship developed that he really could get things done. He knew everyone. He would just pick up the phone and cut right through the bureaucracy. I guess he advised some of the professors and administrators on their personal investments and had some leverage.

We spent a few minutes mapping out the plan. He phoned admissions and got me an appointment that afternoon. By the end of the day, I had my college career mapped out. "Accounting class, then acting class"—that ought to sufficiently screw me up, I thought.

I felt so relieved and comfortable that I knew that I was now doing the right thing.

After semester break, I returned to my new schedule. I took a bunch of required courses plus an accounting course for my major and an improvisation class for my minor.

In January, I acted in a one-act play called "What Did You Learn in School Today?"—a comedic allegory about the goofy board of directors of an imaginary corporation. It was my first comedy, and it was fun working on comic pieces of business. I finished it just as fraternity rush started.

The sixties were the heydays of college fraternities. Fraternities and sororities were the center of the college's social life. If parties and girls were important to you, you had to join a fraternity.

Open-House weekend started the process. There were eight fraternities on campus and each would open its house to interested freshmen. I called this "hypocrisy Sunday." Everyone dressed the same: blue blazer, tan slacks, rep tie, and penny loafers and, of course, the embarrassing beanie. This event gave the fraternities the opportunity to meet the freshmen, while it gave the freshmen a chance to evaluate whether the personality of the fraternities were compatible with theirs.

This was one big farce. The only reason Open-House Sunday was created was to pacify some governmental, politically correct regulation for equal opportunity. The fraternity guys were on their best behavior. They served punch and cookies. With the sincerity of a carnival barker, they shook everyone's hand and welcomed him into the house. After a brief tour, the real prospects were separated from the nerds. The nerds were then herded into the living room and given a long boring paper on the history of fraternity life to read while the real prospects were rushed. The reality was if you were given anything to read and/or seated next to a guy with tape on his glasses or a turban on his head, it was likely you missed the A list.

The real hypocrisy was that by January, 99.9 percent of the pledges were already identified. Most of the A-list guys had more than one bid so the real purpose of open house and the rush period was to get the best guys to join your fraternity. The good guys were assigned a sponsor. He was responsible for introducing the potential pledge to the other brothers, buying beers, and keeping the other fraternities away.

Each fraternity offered approximately twenty to twenty-five bids with the hopes of getting fifteen to twenty pledges. Before the bids were sent out, there was bid night. A meeting was held where each potential pledge was submitted for approval. There would be a brief sales pitch on each candidate, then a secret ballot. Only one black ball was needed to prevent a bid. Rarely was there a surprise. When there was, the secret ballot quickly became public.

The blackballer then had to explain why he voted against the candidate. The reasons were no personality, ugliness, plus a whole list of childish reasons with, "I don't think he'd look good in our jacket," topping the list. Once in a while, there was a legitimate reason like he hit on someone's girlfriend or he was a fag.

After you were notified that you received a bid, you were given a couple of days to accept or reject. I received a few bids, but chose APA because I liked most of the guys. They had the best house, and I liked the blue and white jackets.

Friday was the deadline because that night was the beginning of Hell Week. The first night you were given a pledge pin and pledge book, assigned a big brother to watch over you, and given the rules of pledging:

A pledge must

- Wear his pledge pin on his shirt, sweater, or jacket at all times.

- Carry his pledge book at all times except for Sunday and Saturday night (after 6:30).

- Appear neatly dressed and groomed at all times.

- Wear jacket, dress shirt, and bowtie on Wednesday until after dinner.

- Conduct himself at all times in a gentlemanly manner.

- Address the brothers with proper respect and comply with their reasonable requests.

- Carry matches at all times.

- Not shave his upper lip from the time of pledging until after formal initiation.

- Make a paddle with his name, fraternity name, and year of graduation.

- Be responsible for everything covered in the pledge meetings.

- Attend all duties assigned by brothers (especially the pledge master).

In addition, each pledge was given a hell letter that outlined several tasks that had to be completed by Hell Night. A few examples of hell letter tasks were:

"Secure a manhole cover." This was a euphemism for a woman's sanitary napkin. Most pledges got it, but occasionally a naive or overly zealous pledge would take the request literally and actually steal a manhole cover from the street. One of the great urban legends was that after a pledge had taken the manhole cover from the sidewalk, he covered the hole with a piece of cardboard so that no one would notice it was missing. An elderly lady walking her dog fell in the hole on top of the dog, killing it instantly.

Some of the other sophomoric tasks required were to find a three-cup bra, get a pubic hair from each sorority president, and paint the testicles on the horse in front of the state capitol (blue and white). In addition to the hell letter, each pledge needed to memorize the name, middle name, major, minor, and hometown of each brother and pledge.

At the end of Hell Week was Hell Night. The pledges would assemble at the frat house in the late evening and turn in their pledge books and hell letter results. They were then escorted to the basement and put into a pitch-black room. A loud speaker had been attached to a clock so that in the dark all that was heard was the loud ticking. Every fifteen minutes someone would yell "fire" and a bucket of water was thrown in the room.

The real harassing would begin at midnight. One by one each pledge was called out, accompanied by screams over the loud speaker.

The pledge was then blindfolded and led into a series of rooms. Each room had its own theme. There was one for fake branding, another for haircutting or drinking blood, all designed to emotionally disturb. Following the crazy-making rooms, were the paddling rooms. In these rooms, the pledges were tested on how well they learned each brother's personal information. To help them remember, a whack with the paddle was provided.

The protocol for being paddled was to first "assume the position." This meant to bend over and grab the ankles. After each hit, the pledge was required to say, "Thank you, sir, that was like the gentle wafts of springtime flowing gently over my tender arsehole. May I please have another?"

This all sounds very childish, but at the time it was fun and designed to help bond the pledges to the brothers. About three in the morning, the pledges were given a couple of hours to sleep. The next morning the brothers served the pledges a big breakfast, then divided them in pairs and sent then out on the hell trip. The trip generally consisted of hitchhiking to some location to get the signature of an alumnus. Saturday night the pledges returned and the beer party began. The pledges were now officially brothers, with all the privileges including wearing the jacket.

The fraternity owned a big old, three-story Victorian house. All the rooms on the second and third floors were converted to bedrooms. The fraternity had converted the basement into a cave. One of the early brothers was a theater major and used his set-building skills to build a very clever area with a TV room, a bar room, and a room to make out with your girl. Drinking alcohol and having girls in the house were strictly prohibited by the school and by the "Greek council." Of course, these rules were never followed.

By the spring of my freshman year, I was finally settled. I had my courses set. I was a member of what was considered one of the better fraternities on campus. I still enjoyed my theater friends and acted in stage plays. The only thing missing was that I was still living at home and missed some of the flavor of being on my own on campus.

On the positive side, my home didn't smell of stale beer and old pizza, and my sheets were cleaned and pressed weekly.

26

Caution, I Feel a Lecture Coming On

My first two college years ran relatively smoothly. My decision to major in business and minor in theater turned out to be a good one. I took additional theater courses from my pool of elective requirements and it looked as though I would end up with a double major. As they say, *that with a dime will buy you*…Breaking my rule of going for the grade and learning by osmosis, I actually enjoyed the learning. Although going from the quantitative measurements of business and finance to a class in improvisation took discipline, I would have given new meaning to the practice of "creative accounting" had I chosen that profession.

I worked at Bennie's camp in the summer and at Walsh's in the winter. Even though the school had introduced a token tuition, I still had money in my pocket. The tuition went from zero to $400 per year and the students went berserk.

We made signs, held rallies, and marched on the state capitol. I was even interviewed by the local newspaper. It didn't really seem like a big deal to me but the activists made it sound life-threatening. I was sucked right in. Activists find the emotional hot button of an issue, then exaggerate it beyond reason. It was interesting to watch, and I learned from the experience.

I am convinced that there is a segment of the population who are born with the activist's gene. It is so powerful that it overwhelms reason, produces real images of paranoia, and nourishes the development of conspiracy theories. This was 1964 just before the Vietnam demonstrations, so what I witnessed was a rehearsal of what was to come.

These protest experiences gave me a first-hand look into the psyche of these activists who would eventually march for civil rights, against the wars, and for the poor. At some level, these are all noble causes. My criticism is not that truth or justice should be pursued, but with the lack of balance, maturity, and naivety that dominated the liberal activist's thinking. Unfortunately, we were entering a decade in which radical liberalism would strongly influence every level of our society including the federal and state legislators.

In retrospect, it probably was healthy to evaluate our values and our entitlement programs, even though many of the conclusions drawn were naïve, impractical, and created an equally evil, reverse discrimination. Who were these idealists who made such an impact?

- They were the well-intentioned who believed there was no evil in the world. There were only misguided, deprived people who have views that were simply misunderstood and with whom we should negotiate.

- They were the well-intentioned who wanted to redistribute the wealth in a free enterprise society and show their knowledge of economics by carrying signs that read, "Jobs yes, Profits no!"

- They were the well-intentioned who sought retribution for the injustices of past generations, such as slavery.

- They were the well-intentioned who believed bad behavior is caused by unfortunate external influences and should be treated and tolerated but never punished.

- They were the well-intentioned who wanted to give and control rather than teach.

180

- They were the well-intentioned who expressed their views emotionally, often aggressively, and, when faced with resistance, always personally.

Because their arguments are mostly founded in theory and idealism, they were concentrated mostly in and around the academic communities. They were the angry men and women who had their fists in the air and their heads in the sand.

Even as time passed and changes in culture occurred, their view of the world remained unchanged. They are cultural elitists who carry the burden of the world's inequities. They are valuable because they keep issues in the forefront. They are dangerous because they suck out the good in society while trying to correct the bad. They stir up the poor by convincing them that they are entitled while ensuring that they remain dependent. Personal accountability doesn't exist.

Since the mid-sixties, this liberal philosophy dominated this country's political action. Unfortunately, this forty-year liberal social experiment was a colossal failure. After spending nearly $8 trillion in entitlements since the mid-sixties, the social landscape statistically remains the same.

The only benefactors have been the bureaucrats who run the programs and the political, social, and party leaders who exploit the programs for personal gain.

Fortunately, in the past decade, the country has moved back to the right. America has always been a country of entrepreneurs, a country of rugged individuals with traditional spiritual and social values. It is a country that believes in hard work and personal accountability. This value system is imbedded into the American psyche.

In spite of ancestral origins, our tradition is to assimilate rather than to remain multicultural. This is what differentiates us from the rest of the world. This is what has made us the most productive, the most successful, and the most generous society in the history of the world.

Meanwhile, back in '64, our protests proved to be fruitless. The tuition was instituted and we all survived. The university system in New York flourished, and has since become one of the leading centers of higher education in the country.

I, on the other hand, was still a sophomore and still looking forward to the next beer party.

27

The Play's the Thing

In the summer that ended my second year, I intensified my involvement in the theater. It was theater-in-the-round, where we did Goldoni from commedia dell'arte, Shakespeare, and Molière. In addition to acting, we built sets, located props, painted, and did all-around handy work.

In the fall, I had my first major role in Archibald MacLeish's *JB*. It was a modern-day version of the story of Job. The director, Jarka Burian, had a great influence on my life. Choosing me, a relative novice, to play the title role was a big risk. My reputation of having one foot in the Theater Department and one in the Business Department, while wearing a fraternity jacket, didn't exactly reflect an undying commitment to the theater. I had worked with him once before playing a few minor roles in Marlowe's *Faustus,* but never anything this big. The entire second act of *JB* was filled with dramatic monologues where God tests Job's loyalty. Adding to my intimidation, the play was to be performed in a Presbyterian Church.

The church was a cathedral—a large gothic structure with a high vaulted ceiling and large stained-glass windows lining the walls. Wooden platforms were built from the altar over the altar rail nearly to the first pew. Each level represented a different scene. It was an impressive sight. We rehearsed in the evenings. The church, the set, and dim lights gave off eerie shadows, adding a strange intensity to the experience, and to my commitment. In addition, there were stories about actors who previously played the role and met with strange accidents. For example, Pat Hingle, who played the role on Broadway, allegedly fell down an elevator shaft.

It was intense. Jarka spent weeks working with me, one on one. We rehearsed the monologue for delivery and articulation. The cathedral, because of its high ceilings and hard surfaces, created special challenges for the actor. Dr. Burian would stand at the back of the church and yell, "I can't hear your Ts."

Of all the plays, this one was the most mentally distracting. I would dream about not knowing what page I was on or falling off the platform. Opening night I had real butterflies. Standing in the vestibule of the church with the house lights at their dimmest and the echoes of the audience's chatter bouncing off the walls created a strangely different mood than I had ever experienced in the theater. The stage lights snapped on as the sound of our footsteps rang out as we entered stage right. I looked down at the audience. It felt as though we were about perform from the top of a mountain. Finally, my voice broke the tension, and I was relieved that I felt the same rush that I had that first time on stage.

In spite of my fears, the performances had only a few insignificant problems. Each night my confidence grew. I became more relaxed. By the end of the two-week run, I couldn't wait for the curtain to rise to play to the sold-out church. The reviews were excellent. The critics loved the church setting, Burian's interpretations, and, luckily, my performance. More importantly, Dr. Burian had instilled a confidence that served me far beyond my theatrical needs.

In the spring I auditioned for a play put on by the City's Civic Theater Group. It was a Molière play entitled *The Imaginary Invalid*. I played a dandy, complete with lipstick, a periwig, stockings, a fluffy shirt, and a handkerchief that I waved as I spoke. I sang a silly song that exaggerated the feminine requirements of the role:

> *Beautiful shepherdess, I, I, I adore you.*
> *Never shepherd was so true.*
> *Tell me. Tell me I, I, I implore you.*
> *Do you love me?*
> *Yes, I l love you, oh so true.*
>
> *This joy is more than I can bear!*
> *I walk on air tra, la, la, la!*
> *I walk on air tra, la, la, la!*

I mention this not because I was uncomfortable with the role, but because of all the roles that I played, this was the only play that my mother chose to bring my grandmother and Aunt Margaret. This was only important because they had been trying to get me married since I started college.

Their approach was always the same. Aunt Margaret and Uncle "Tony, the tailor" had no children. Every year, they would import a young girl from their hometown in Italy. It was usually a country girl in her late teens. The girl would work for my aunt as a housekeeper/cook for about a year. This was just long enough to satisfy the immigration department's Green Card requirements.

They were usually very pretty—in a primitive way. Coming from Italy's agricultural south, they were dark, could cook, and looked as though they could beat me up. They spoke no English and had little exposure to American culture other than the belief that the streets were paved with gold. After the year of this indentured servitude, the ladies would start the husband hunt. Since I was single and a college boy, I was a prime target. It would start like this.

"Your Aunt Margaret and grandmother want to see you," my mother would announce.

"And why is that, Ma?"

"They need some help with the storm windows."

"Storms windows? It's only July. Are they expecting snow?"

"Don't be smart. Just go over and help. They have been very good to you."

"Good to me? A glass of ginger ale and two dollars in an envelope for my birthday?"

"It's not the amount, it's the thought."

"They've imported another one, haven't they?" I said.

"I don't know."

"What's her name?"

"Maria, I think."

"They're all named Maria."

"Not true, there was a Josephine two years ago. Don't argue with me. Just go! I don't ask much. Do this for me."

I learned a long time ago not to argue about the little stuff. Especially with the, *I don't ask much*, preface. I wasn't going to win the argument, so why bother trying? The next day I made the visit.

As I entered my aunt's house, my grandmother and aunt were sitting on the couch. They were dressed in the usual navy blue polka-dot house dress, laced square-heeled shoes, heavy nylons with their arms crossed resting on their enormous boobs. I walked over and gave them the customary, mandatory kiss and received the usual *que bella* cheek squeeze.

"What's up, girls?"

"You getta more handsome every day! How's you mother?" my aunt asked, ignoring my question.

"My mother's fine. She said something about storm windows."

"Forget abouta the windows!" Yelling toward the kitchen, "Hey, Maria, vene qua!"

Out of the kitchen carrying a tray of cheese, salami, and peppers comes Maria with a big smile. She looked like the last one only a little taller and with a little more hair on her legs. In all fairness, they always had nice tits.

"Maria, (in Italian) this is my grandson Carlo. He is a college boy. He knows everything. He's gonna be a teacher."

"I'm not going to be a teacher, but I do know everything." (Why make her insecure?)

"Hey, what'sa difference? Say hello to Maria. She comes from the town right next to your grandfather—a very good family. She's cooks and cleans beautifully. Isn't she pretty?"

"Yes, she is. Hi, Maria."

She walks toward me and asks, *"Que causa mangiare?"*

"No, thank you, I have already eaten. No English, Grandma?"

"She will learn very quickly. Here sit, talk. We'll be in the kitchen."

Our conversation lasted about two minutes. My Italian consisted of about twenty words and maybe two sentences. Her English was even more limited. After greetings and the usual, "How do you like America?" I was finished. I used to ask about a blow job until I got caught by one of them who spoke more English than she let on.

Having done my duty, I left with the promise I would return. Surprisingly, every girl who was brought over was married within a couple of years—a remarkable record for a couple of old ladies who could barely speak English.

Now these two ladies were sitting in the audience of a seventeenth-century drawing room comedy watching their prime marriage candidate prancing around like a true *finocchio*!

After the play, we retired to my grandmother's kitchen for coffee and Stella Dora's anisette sponges. My grandmother kept looking at me. Finally, she leaned over and asked, "Hey, Carlucci, how coma you dressa up like a girl with the lipastick anda wig?

"Grandma, it's acting. That's what the role required. It's called a costume."

"I dunnooo! I think a theresa something wrong with you whooo!" she sang.

I turned to my mother in desperation and said, "Help!"

I think Grandma was very relieved when I got married a few years later. Even though my wife was 5-foot-7, blonde, blue-eyed with ancestors who came over on the Mayflower, Grandma never complained.

Tony the Tailor and Margarita the matchmaker

28

Sgt. Gudermoothe, Then the Curtain Falls

By graduation I had some big decisions to make. The Vietnam War had heated up, and there was no way to beat the draft but to move to Canada. I also had to decide whether I would pursue the theater professionally or enter the business world.

Since Canada was out of the question, in April of my senior year I visited the Air Force recruitment center. I picked the Air Force because I felt I would rather get shot out of the air than get blown up in a muddy foxhole. The recruiter, Sgt. Gudermoothe, was a real friendly guy.

All recruiters are either from the South, or they faked a Southern accent. I have yet to meet one who called the Bronx his home. Gudermoothe was a good old boy who was a career noncom and who answered every question as if he were reading it out of a manual. I told him I went to military school so that I understood the basic stuff, but I wanted to fly.

Apparently recruiting pilots was a big deal, or he got a special bonus, like every Wednesday off, because his eyes lit up. Little did I know that my interest would turn on a thirty-minute presentation on the benefits of being an Air Force officer.

"If you qualified, Uncle Sam would be investing hundreds of thousands on your training," he proudly announced. It was as if I had wound him up. He went on and on.

Finally, I said, "Okay, you convinced me. Where do I sign?"

"Well, sir, first you have to take an exam to determine whether you have the intelligence to fly." He was already calling me sir. I liked that!

He scheduled the exam the following week. It took several hours and consisted of the usual IQ stuff plus a section on reading maps and finding things in aerial photographs. It was actually pretty tough.

A few days later, Gudermoothe called me to congratulate me on passing.

"You're almost home, son."

Son, I thought, *what happened to sir?*

He went on, "All that is left is a simple preliminary draft physical. We'll then sign the papers and you'll be off to Texas."

The draft physical was held at the combined recruitment office downtown. It was a zoo. There were at least a hundred guys milling around. No one seemed too happy.

The registration desk was located right at the door with a big Enlistment/Draft Physical sign and was manned by representatives of each branch of the service. I gave my name, and I immediately enjoyed discrimination at its best. The sergeant at the desk looked up and smiled. "Welcome, sir, you're an OCS candidate. Please step into the room on the right."

Well, this is every civilized, I thought. Meanwhile, the nice guy behind me was a draftee. He was sent to the room on the left, minus the welcome and the sir.

The Officer Candidate School (OCS) candidate room had a long table with about a dozen chairs and a water cooler in the corner. By the time everyone registered, there were less than ten of us in the room.

The room across the hall was filled with draftees. It was noisy and unruly. The sergeants were shouting orders and generally being abusive. The OCS room was the antithesis. The sergeant came in and announced that we would be processed first and to let him know if there were any questions—all very polite, all very respectful.

It took about an hour to get through the physical. At the end, both draftees and OCS candidates lined up in our shorts for a final inspection.

A tall, skinny corporal, who was earlier introduced as the "coreman," walked down the long line eyeballing each candidate from head to toe. Stopping in front of me, he looked down, then up, down again, then up again.

"Are you aware, sir, that you have *pes pauper?*"

"*Pes pauper?*" I repeated. This guy can hardly speak English and he's using his Latin on me. "I'm sorry but I'm not familiar with the term *pes pauper.*"

"Bad feet," he explained smugly.

"Oh yes, low arches. I was born that way," I replied.

"Do they bother you?" He asked, looking me in the eye as if he had the skill of a lie detector.

"Not that I can remember. I do remember when I was young my parents tried to help with foot arches but finally gave up."

Not only did I *not* have a problem, but I played basketball for hours several days a week without the slightest discomfort.

"Are you trying to be a hero?"

"Not about my feet," I said.

"Go in that door and report to the major. He's the doc on duty." He handed me my file and pointed to an office down the line.

As I walked down the line, I saw people holding X-rays. Some were coughing, others were moaning. They were all looking for an excuse to get out. I, on the other hand, was in the best shape of my life: 6 foot, 1 inch, 175 pounds, and was resigned to the idea of spending a few years in the military.

I walked right up to the major's desk. He was smoking a pipe and looked a little disheveled.

"The corporal told me to see you, Major," I said.

He looked up at me over his glasses. "Did he say what for?"

"Pes pauper," I replied.

"Pes pauper?" He stood up, leaned over his desk down at my feet.

"He's right, *pes pauper.* Do they bother you?"

"No!"

"Are you trying to be a hero?"

"Look, Major, I am enlisting to fly airplanes not to march to Saigon."

"You still have basic training and it could evolve into a permanent disability, costing the tax payer dearly. Hand me your file."

He took the file and began writing. "One Y. I am reclassifying you to One Y."

"What does that mean?" I asked

"It means that you're kind of…on hold. If we need you, we'll call. In the meantime, get dressed and go home."

I turned, and walked out of the office past the line of the draftees with their X-rays. I got dressed, but instead of going home, I thought that I'd see Gudermoothe. I was really disappointed and a little depressed. I was a reject and I felt crushed. That was until the light bulb in my head flashed on. I was not going into the service or going to Vietnam.

I was free!! By the time I got to Gudermoothe's office, a smile was beginning to etch itself on to my face.

"Bad news, Sergeant," I said in my best acting voice.

Gudermoothe's face dropped. "What is it?"

"I failed the physical."

"Oh no, I'm sorry. Was it a heart problem?"

"No, *pes pauper*."

"*Pes pauper, pes pauper,* nobody gets out for *pes pauper*. I've had *pes pauper* for twenty-seven years." He took off his shoes and started jumping up and down. "Show me your papers."

I handed him the paper that they gave me before I left.

"One Y, One Y for *pes pauper*. You can protest—a simple letter to your congressman."

"Good idea, Sergeant, but right now I want to be alone," sounding like Garbo.

"I understand."

Head bowed, I left the office. I walked slowly until I got to the elevator. The door opened and I entered. The door closed and it was Showtime. I started dancing and singing the song from Gypsy, "*Everything's coming up roses.*"

I was hard to believe, but by enlisting I had avoided the draft right in the middle of the war. I later found out that this was luck. Each draft board had a quota. The closer they were to their quota, the stricter they were in enforcing military physical regulations. It was the end of the month, and Albany had already made its quota. The perfect storm!

The rest of the semester, I was in heaven. I never realized what a weight the impending draft had on me. A few weeks later I received my revised draft card with the One Y classification. Who knows how different my life would have been had I gone?

Graduation was surprisingly uneventful. We had a small get-together with the family, took a few pictures, and it was over—nothing like the high school bash.

I took a job with an insurance company as a claims adjuster. My salary was $6,000 per year plus a car. It was a white Mercury Comet with no options. I told everyone that I was an insurance investigator because it sounded better. Unfortunately, the only things I ever investigated were broken windows, small fender-benders, and homeowner claims.

I hated the job until I understood how much power that I had. I could either pay the claim, deny it, or lose the paperwork. It became fun when I realized that I could take care of the good people and screw the hustlers. The old ladies and poor people always got paid generously, while the sharpie, lawyer types had to cross every *t* and dot every *i*. I felt like Robin Hood.

Sometimes I would help out with a claim. For example, in order to get paid for property stolen from your car, there had to be a physical sign of forcible entry. This poor elderly woman had her camera and purse taken from her car while she was at the doctor's. The thief either jimmied the lock or—more likely—the woman forgot to lock her car. I told her about the sign of forced entry and that I was going for coffee down the street. When I returned, all the side windows were smashed. I smiled and said, "The vent window would have been sufficient." She was so proud of herself! I paid her the max! Case closed.

A few months later, I was driving past the airport. I thought that working for the airlines might be fun. I pulled into the parking lot and entered the main terminal. I checked out all the airlines, but picked American because I liked the logo.

I was directed back to the offices. A pleasant man with bushy, white hair asked if he could be of help. I mentioned my interest in working for the airline, and he invited me back to his office. Luckily, as I found out later, I was talking to the city manager, the most senior guy at the location. We talked and joked for about an hour. If it was an interview, I didn't realize it until it was over. He asked me to complete an application and told me that he would let me know if any openings became available.

I left the airport feeling pretty good. Two days later, I was called in and interviewed by the HR person and the regional vice president, who happened to be visiting the airport. When it was over, they provisionally offered me the position of "management understudy." It was a new training program that had just been introduced for college graduates who wanted to pursue a career in airline management. They said they had to check my references before a formal offer could be extended.

The next day I left, with my friend Kevin, for New York to see some plays and to talk to a few actors he knew. We arrived Saturday morning about 11 AM. We walked from the bus terminal on 8th to the Holiday Inn on Broadway where we shared a $15 room.

It was great year for theater in New York. We walked to the *twofer* trailer on 46th and got tickets for *Royal Hunt of the Sun,* the story of the Incas and Pizarro. The Spanish explorer Pizarro captures the Inca god-chief Atahualpa and promises to free him upon the deliverance of a horde of gold. A great play with colorful, bigger-than-life sets, and a jaw-dropping characterization of the Sun god by Christopher Plummer.

Later, we got tickets for *Marat Sade,* whose complete title was *The Persecution and Assassination of Jean-Paul Marat as Performed by the Inmates of the Asylum of Charenton Under the Direction of the Marquis de Sade.* It was wonderfully performed by the Royal Shakespearean Company and directed by Peter Brooks. One of its claims to fame was that it was the first time nudity was shown on Broadway.

Quite tame by today's standards, it consisted of Marat, who spent the entire play in a bathtub because it was the only relief for his rare skin disease, getting up and walking across the stage naked. It is hard to believe that it was considered so avant-garde.

Whenever I see great theater, I get excited and motivated to act. Choosing the life of a professional actor was still very much on my mind. The desire would ebb and flow depending on how secure I was feeling the time. Seeing these great plays really got me excited about the idea.

Late Saturday night, we had arranged to meet Willie, a friend of Kevin's. Willie had been the star of a children's TV show in Albany about ten years earlier. He moved to New York to attend the American Academy of Dramatic Arts. This was the school for serious actors with an alumni consisting of world-class notables.

Willie lived on West 57th Street in a small apartment with his wife and young son. New York apartment living is intimidating if you don't understand and love the New York City lifestyle. The building was old, and the walk-up apartment was small. Willie was very friendly and positive. He drove a cab to support himself and his family. Cab driving was a great job for an actor because it provided the flexibility to audition.

He was just coming off duty, but we first drove to Downey's, an Irish bar in the heart of the theater district. The place was a hangout for actors, writers, and other theatrical types.

We grabbed a table and ordered Irish coffees.

We talked for a while about the theater and the plays we had just seen. I was trying to impress him with my knowledge of the theater and its history. I was not very good at playing the artsy intellectual type. Finally, I admitted that my real reason for talking to him was that I wanted to pursue acting professionally, and I needed some advice from someone who was actually doing it.

He asked me about what I had done and where. I told him mostly college and some summer and civic theater.

"Very impressive," he said, trying not to sound patronizing. "You have a great voice."

"Thanks."

"Do you love acting?"

"Sure."

"No. I asked, do you LOVE acting?"

"Sure."

"I'm not trying to be overly dramatic, but if you don't really love it, this is a hard, shitty way to live."

I smiled, "I know it's not easy."

"Look," leaning toward me. "I have been here for nearly ten years. I have a wife and a little boy. I love them very much. New York is expensive. You saw the apartment. That's all that I can afford. I work six days a week driving the cab. I still go to class and I audition whenever I can. I still don't know when or if I'm gong to make it."

"Hey man, you have great credentials."

"Don't mean a fucking thing," getting more intense. "All my experience and all your experience together won't buy a cup of coffee. Every audition is like coming out of the gate for the first time. It's arbitrary and cruel. You're too tall, too short, too dark, not dark enough, you're not good looking, you're too good looking—the list is endless. If you're not tough, it will eat you right up!"

"You don't make it sound like it's much fun."

"It's not…and it is. If you don't love it and don't really believe in yourself, forget it. On the other hand, I can't imagine doing anything else. It might happen tomorrow, or next year, or in another ten years, but I am one hundred percent convinced that I will make it."

I sat there reeling from his directness.

"Look, I don't mean to scare you but I don't want to mislead you, either. If you want to do it, I applaud your courage. Let me know and I will help you any way I can, but remember, you must be tenacious, better yet, chauvinistic—fanatically prejudiced in the belief of your superiority." He leaned back and smiled, "I gotta get the cab back. Enjoy your stay." He got up and left.

Kevin and I sat there for another hour talking about what he had said. I couldn't sleep that night. Intentionally or not, he had scared me. Not fair—he didn't scare me as much as he made me focus. He was right on target about devotion and I knew it.

The next morning we had a big breakfast at one those Times Square, carnival-looking restaurants. As we walked to the bus terminal, it became overcast, chilly, and was starting to rain. We got on the bus and Kevin fell asleep almost immediately. I stared out the window watching as the day darkened and the rain increased. I must have fallen asleep, because I didn't notice our pulling into the Albany bus terminal. We grabbed our bags, and as we walked out of the dark station, the sun broke through the clouds. Coincidentally, an airplane flew overhead.

On Monday, I accepted the job with American Airlines. I never looked back.

Willie went on to become a star on TV and in the movies—his name, William Devane. I'm sure he doesn't remember me, or the dramatic effect he had on my life.

29

Check Your Bag, Sir?

Having temporarily set aside my histrionic ambitions, I began my airline career. In those days, working for the airlines was considered a real prize. Airline travel was still only being used by a small percentage of the population and was still glamorous. The airlines were strictly regulated so that price wars were nonexistent. There were no frequent flier mile clubs or other free fare programs. In fact, giving away an airline seat was illegal. The government regulated tariffs, routes, and virtually everything the airlines did. It was a happy time because everyone was making money. The big names no longer around were PanAm, Eastern, Braniff, Mohawk, Frontier, and in California, PSA.

Airline marketing focused on growing the industry and getting people interested in flying rather than building market share. The industry played off its glamorous image by hiring the most beautiful women they could find for their flight attendants. At that time, they were called stewardesses and they were all women. They had strict image requirements and had to retire on their 32nd birthday. Dating a stewardess was the equivalent of dating a model. Service was king.

From serving coffee and Danish in the boarding lounge to carving chateaubriand at your seat, each airline tried to outdo the other with the amenities they provided their passengers. The larger airplanes had lounges with pianos. Meals served in the coach cabin were better than what is served in first class today. For the business travelers, they built luxury clubs at the airport where special boarding privileges were provided along with free drinks, coffee, and snacks. The clubs had names like The Admirals, the Presidents, The Crown Room, or the Red Carpet Club.

This was all done with the objective of convenience, personal attention, enhancing the glamour of the flying experience with the ultimate objective of growing the entire market.

Working for the airlines was like joining a fraternity. We not only socialized with fellow employees, but with the competition. Each airline had an interline department devoted to providing benefits to the competition. The objective was to get your competition to recommend your airline on non-competitive routes. To that end, the interline-fam-trip was created.

A "fam" or interline familiarization trip was a three- to ten-day vacation exclusively for airline personnel. It was ridiculously cheap. For example, four days in the Virgin Islands including airfare, hotel, and meals for only $49, or ten days in Africa on a picture-taking safari, all inclusive, for only $149. It was a great way to see the world without being rich. It was one of the biggest attractions of working in the industry.

We flew standby, and if you didn't get on a flight, many times someone at the airport would invite you home to sleep on the couch. In addition to the passes, once a year the industry held the international, interline Christmas party in Las Vegas. It started December 1st and ran for twelve straight days. The discounted hotel room was $5 per night. Each night a different airline would sponsor a party, one trying to outdo the other. No one stayed for the twelve days. Most people collapsed after two or three. The drinks were free, the food was great, and the women were plentiful. Even the crippled elevator operator got laid.

It was into this incredible world that I stumbled. I had been selected for American Airlines' management understudy program, a program designed to develop airline management skills. For six months each understudy would work and learn the various functions at the airport.

I started with checking bags and learning all the airline codes. Next, I moved to the ticket counter where I learned to use the reservation system called Sabre and how to calculate fares and write tickets.

The next stop was fleet service where I learned cargo tariffs and how the plane was loaded and emptied. The final training areas were operations to learn load balancing and the gate.

At the gate, I checked in passengers for the flight, went out on the ramp, and with two lit batons actually waved the plane to a stop, placed the chocks under the wheels and deplaned the passengers. This was before they installed Jet-ways. At the conclusion of the training, I was made a first-line supervisor.

The only real negative other than the strange hours was the uniform. It was a blue suit, a military style hat, and a name tag. I was once told that if you turned thirty and you were still wearing a name tag, your career was in trouble. Forget my age: it bothered me to wear a name tag.

Unfortunately, my career became troubled almost immediately after I finished training. It was the dead of winter when I became manager on duty. In the small airports, the supervisor ran the shift. This meant that the skycaps, ticket agents, operation and fleet service all reported to the M.O.D. For someone who had never flown or had even been in an airport before his appointment, this was an awesome responsibility.

I worked the late-shit shift: 3 PM to 11 PM, Wednesdays to Sundays with Mondays and Tuesdays off. Since Albany was a diversion city, the airport never closed at 11 PM. Diversion meant if there was a weather problem in New York, Boston. or Buffalo, the airplane was sent to us.

Albany was a very senior operation. This meant that most of the staff had been around more than a decade. They were all experienced and, in spite of the regular disruptions, the operation usually ran smoothly. Knowing that I was wet behind the ears, the senior guys played pranks on me whenever they could. Everyone was in on the joke, including the pilots.

We were flying turbo props in those days, Lockheed 188s, or "Electras," as they were called. The 9 PM flight had just landed. I put the chocks on the wheels and plugged into the plane to talk to the pilot.

"Welcome to Albany," I said in my new official voice.

"Are you the new M.O.D.?" the captain replied.

"Yes, sir, I am. What can I do for you?"

"How long are we on the ground?"

"Forty-five minutes, sir."

"Look, we have been experiencing some drag on the left propeller. We think it might be dirt build-up. Would you get some prop wash and get someone clean it off?"

"Prop wash?" Not having the slightest idea what he was talking about. "I think we have some. Let me check."

"You better hurry. We don't want to be delayed."

I dropped the earphones and ran into Operations.

"Hey, Harry. The pilot needs prop wash. Do we have any?"

Harry, looking very serious while shaking head, "I think I saw a 5-gallon container in fleet service. Ask Billy, he's out on the ramp."

I ran back on the ramp: "Billy, we need prop wash. Harry said there was a container in fleet."

"Yes, right inside the door. It looks like a red gas can. It's light but be careful, it's very combustible. If you get it, we'll apply it."

I ran about 100 yards to the hangar. Sure enough, to the right of the fleet service door was a red container. I picked it up. It *was* very light. I carefully carried it back to the plane. Standing by the cargo door, with their backs to me, were the pilot, co-pilot, the fleet service supervisor, Billy and Harry from Operations.

"Hey, guys, I found it. I got the prop wash! Come on, we only have fifteen minutes," I said, breathing heavily from all the running.

They all turned, started laughing and clapping. "Congratulations," the pilot said, "you just fell for the oldest prank in the book. I can't believe it still works. Prop wash is the wind that is produced by the propeller."

There I stood, out of breath and stupid. They walked over, shook my hand, and welcomed me aboard.

After a few a days of ribbing about the prop wash, they let me off the hook. Handling storms and disgruntled passengers was initially very stressful. After a while, I adapted and learned to take it all in stride. It is, however, a way to quickly create a close bond with your fellow workers. It was like going to battle rather than to a job. Because of the strange hours, often after work, we'd go out for a few drinks or for breakfast. It is generally not a good idea to socialize with people who work for you, but in this case it seemed very natural.

Within a couple of months, I was a veteran. The more comfortable I became, the more creatively I handled problems. The crew liked it because I never hid in the back room. I was always out front when there was a problem. I was, however, often getting into trouble with the management. Many times when passengers were diverted, we put them into hotels, got buses to move them, or just fed them. I was pretty loose with the company's money. If a plane were delayed for a couple of hours, I'd give everyone "chits" and send them to the bar. Most times that would sweeten them up. Sometimes it would make them meaner.

The two incidents most responsible for the end of my career in airport operations involved a de-icer and a plow.

When it snowed and a plane sat too long on the ramp, ice built up on the wings. The ice affected lift and therefore was dangerous. Sometimes the propeller would bleed it off, but most of the time a de-icer was needed to melt the ice. Because Albany was a small operation for American, Mohawk Airlines handled our maintenance.

We had an Electra on the ramp during a snowstorm when the pilot requested a de-icing. I called Mohawk and they promised they'd be over immediately. A half hour passed and no Mohawk. I called again.

The plane was already delayed and everyone was getting pissed at me. I went on board and authorized the stewardess to break open the liquor kit. I called Mohawk again but no one answered. I put on my coat and cap and ran over to the Mohawk operation area. The ramp was empty but there sitting alone on the ramp was the de-icer. A de-icer is a small truck with a cherry-picking arm. I walked over and saw that the keys were in the ignition. It was one of those moments where something illogical seems logical.

I started the truck and drove it over to the American side of the ramp. I grabbed one of the fleet service guys and put him into the cherry picker, and, with a little difficulty, I raised the arm. Finally, we started spraying the plane. We finished in about fifteen minutes. The plane took off. I drove the truck back only to be met by the officious Mohawk maintenance manager. He was still yelling when I was walked away.

I was called into the city manger's office the next day where, during a thirty-minute lecture, I was made familiar with the many policies and laws that I had broken. The regional VP, Otto Becker, said he appreciated my dilemma and applauded my resourcefulness, but indicated how quickly my career would end if it happened again.

Three weeks later, I arrived at the job in the middle of another snowstorm. There were planes on the ground and people all over the airport.

If I could have gone home, I would have. The airport was a mess: planes on the ramp, people crowded into the lounges, and it was only 3 PM. I walked into Operations and the day manger stood up, put on his coat, wished me luck, and left. We had delays, diversions, and cancellations. The ramp and ticket counter people already looked exhausted and their shift had just started.

Luckily, about 6 PM the snow stopped and the weather was blowing to the north. If I could only get the runways cleared, I could clean up this mess. I called the county and asked about the plows. They told me two were down and two were working. It was then that the illogical seemed logical to me again.

My cousin Sal had a construction company but had a contract in the winter to plow the streets. I called and offered him $200 to buy an hour of two of his trucks. He said he'd do it as a favor. I told him to make sure there was no salt in the trucks. I knew the salt was bad for the planes.

I went down to the ticket counter and took the money out of the cash drawers, and replaced it with an IOU. I met the trucks at the gate and told the guard what we were doing. He let them in. I told them just to follow the county trucks.

In less than an hour, one runway was clear. The trucks left and within the hour so did the planes. By 11 PM, the airport was clear. I was so pleased with myself that I went out and drank a few…well, a few too many.

The next day, as I walked through the terminal, I could feel the staff staring at me. As I entered Operations, I was directed into the city manager's office. I was a little hung over so I wasn't picking up the subtleties.

In the city manager's office sat Abby Roland, the city manager, and Otto Becker, the regional vice president. The two of them just stared at me.

"Hi," I said awkwardly.

Waving a piece of paper, "The auditor said he found this with the ticket counter receipts." Abby continued, "It says, 'I owe American Airlines two hundred dollars.'"

"And I have a complaint from the county that says someone allowed two unauthorized vehicles on the airport runway," Otto interrupted.

"Oh, I can explain everything," I said.

The door closed, and the lectures began and ended with, "The only reason that we don't fire you on the spot and fine you is that you cleared out the airport. Miraculously, you took care of the passengers. You were lucky, not smart. You're a loose cannon, and we're sorry to tell you that your career in airport operations has ended."

I had just blown a great job, I thought. I turned and started out the door.

"Wait," Mr. Becker motioned for me to sit down.

"I know this is a blow to you, but we have no choice. You have managed to piss off not only the county but Mohawk, our local ground maintenance partner. We have no choice but to relieve you of your duties."

"I understand."

"I do have an option for you. I have spoken to Al Ackerman, the sales manager in Boston. He has an opening for a sales rep, if you're interested."

Trying not to show my excitement, "Oh, that sounds interesting."

"Good, why don't you fly over tomorrow? I can only recommend. The final decision is his."

"Thank you, Mr. Becker, I really appreciate all you have done to help me out."

Wow, what a swing, I thought. I can't believe I went from being fired to my dream job in minutes. Airline Sales Rep had to be the best job on the planet! Normal hours, a pay raise, and no more uniform and name tag. I think this is called percussive sublimation, or getting kicked upstairs.

I flew to Boston the next day, had a great interview, and was offered the job. When I returned that evening, I saw Abby in the terminal. He came over to congratulate me.

"We're going to miss you. You weren't so bad. A loose cannon, but not so bad."

The staff threw me little going-away party, and I was off to Boston—after a two-day hangover. It was a pretty good party.

30

All Work and No play

One of the great benefits of working on a shift is the ability to swap schedules. This was particularly important when your most valued fringe benefit was free travel. My schedule was Wednesday to Sunday with Monday and Tuesday off. If I swapped Monday and Tuesday, I could get four days off for a short trip or two Mondays and Tuesdays for a six day and a longer trip.

During my first year at American, I was able to travel to Mexico, the Virgin Islands, California, and Florida. Not bad considering that before this I had never been on an airplane. The travel was so exciting that I didn't care if I was checking bags, wearing a uniform, or even working the night shift. I was only making $7500 per year but was living like $75,000.

My first real trip was to Acapulco. I convinced Abby, my manager, that as part of my training I needed to learn more about how the product was delivered in other cities and countries. He knew that I was full of shit but he gave me a Class C pass anyway, which was standby business class. This gave me boarding priority over a Class D or vacation pass. This was important when going to a busy destination.

I left Albany for Chicago on the 8 AM flight in my first first-class seat. We had a nice breakfast, washed down with orange juice and champagne—a mimosa I think it was called. In those days, we were required to wear a coat and tie when traveling on a pass.

The gate for the Chicago/Acapulco was overrun with people. I went to the counter and asked about availability.

"Hi, I'm Carl. I work out of Albany. How does it look for standby?"

The pretty girl behind the counter made a face. "It looks tight, Carl. We're overbooked by five, and I have six standbys. "Overbooked" is different from "oversold." Oversold mean people are left at the gate, while overbooked means that the forecasting system made provisions for no-shows. Travel agents block seats and often don't release them.

I handed her my pass.

"Oh, Class C. You'll get on. I'm not sure that I can get you up front, but I'll try."

Flying standby is nerve-wracking, because you don't know until the very last minute whether you'll get on. As the passengers checked in, I stood close but out of the way.

She began calling the standbys. "Johnson, Russell, Barnaby..." I began to panic. I was the only one left in the lounge. Finally, she called my name.

"Congratulations, you got the only first-class seat. The rest are in the back."

My pass had just jumped me over the other standbys. I felt bad but not too bad and only for a few seconds.

"You're the best. If I can ever return the favor..." I gave her my card as if that meant anything. She wasn't bad looking. Who knows? I was always mining in those days.

I boarded the plane, sat in a big, comfortable first-class seat and was handed a glass of champagne. If Clods, Dirty Hands, and Louie could only see me now.

The service was spectacular. Fresh caesar salad, prime rib, cut from the cart, and one of the greatest hot fudge sundaes I'd ever had—of course, there was unlimited booze. I watched a little bit of the movie and fell asleep.

The next thing I heard was, "Please return your tray tables and seats to an upright position and prepare for landing."

Arriving in a foreign country for the first time is like a dream. It doesn't feel real. The sights and smells were different. It was the first time I had seen palm trees and experienced the feel of tropical weather. I was like a little kid discovering a new world.

I passed customs and grabbed a shuttle for the thirty-minute trip to the hotel. I couldn't believe that I was actually in Acapulco. My first sight of the ocean was really my first sight of any ocean. There were no oceans in upstate New York. The high-rise hotels hugged the white sand that framed the horseshoe-shaped bay. The sight was breathtaking.

I had reservations at the El Presidente Hotel located right on the beach. The hotel was one of American's travel partners so that the airline employee rate was about only about 50 pesos or about $12 per day. The lobby was bright, shiny white, and black marble with views to the ocean. I checked into my room, got into my bathing suit, and went straight to the pool. There was a pool-side bar with a thatched roof made of straw where I stopped and had a piña colada.

Next to me sat a beautiful Hispanic girl in a bikini that left nothing to the imagination. Long straight black hair, green eyes, and the whitest teeth I'd ever seen. I was in Acapulco for five minutes and already in love. I was trying to think of something witty, when she turned, smiled, and said, "Hello."

"Hello to you. Boy, what a beautiful sight."

"The bay is beautiful this time of day," she said with a slight accent.

"The bay, too," I said. "Are you visiting?"

"Yes, we got here a few days ago."

"From?" *This is too easy,* I thought.

"Buenos Aires."

"I'm Carlo." I thought I'd use my baptized name. It seemed more continental. *This was too easy,* I thought.

"Lisa," she said, as she shook my hand. "You're American?" (So much for the Carlo stuff.)

"Yes, I…" Just as I was about to get in gear, a tall, Hispanic-looking, handsome guy walked up, kissed her on the check, and said with a heavy accent, "Come on, Lisa, we're going to Paradisio for shrimp."

"I have to go. Nice meeting you." She got up and headed toward the beach. I found out later that Paradisio was a beach-side restaurant famous for its garlic barbecued shrimp, and a very "in" place.

Brief but exciting, I thought. I knew it couldn't be that easy. Disappointed, but not discouraged. I relaxed by the pool for the next few hours. I still thought I was dreaming.

That night, I had dinner at the hotel and few drinks at the bar. I was really exhausted. I went to my room for a nap, fell asleep immediately, and didn't wake until the next morning.

I was told that as an American Airlines' employee, I should introduce myself to the sales department when the hotel is a travel partner. After all, the point of the "fam" trip and the special rate was to promote the hotel and destination as a means of promoting the airline. That morning I met the sales manager, Manuel Olaiz—a very charming guy, about my age, with perfect English. He was a graduate of UCLA, and his mannerisms and speech patterns were more American than Mexican.

We walked down to the restaurant for breakfast. He told me how much he loved L.A. and the States. It wasn't long before we were becoming friends. When I asked him about the nightlife and the hip places to go, he offered to show me around.

In those days, I loved to play tennis. Where, would you ask, would an inner city kid learn to play such a preppy game, especially then, before it became so popular? To answer that question, we need to leave Acapulco for a moment and return to Albany.

Just after graduation, when I worked as an insurance adjustor, I left the office in the morning and didn't return until the next day. I was allegedly settling claims. The great thing about the job was there was little supervision. Many days I would be finished by 3 PM. Eventually, I regularly worked five-hour days—not a demanding job.

One Friday morning, I was settling a smoke damage claim in one of the brownstones on Washington Avenue bordering the city's main park. When I finished, I walked to the park to watch the tennis players. I had never watched tennis before. A couple of great-looking girls in short white skirts first caught my attention, but it was the sophisticated, gentle, yet aggressive flavor that intrigued me. I didn't know why, but I knew I needed to learn this game.

The next morning I bought a pair of white shorts, a tennis racket, and some balls. I returned to the courts that afternoon and began asking people to play. Everyone, including the kids, rejected me.

Discouraged, I sat on the bench and watched the players on the first court. There appeared to be a pecking order with the first few courts reserved for the better players. I sat for about an hour watching. I was hoping to pick up some tips on how the game was played.

"Have you been watching the Open?" A voice came from an adjoining bench. I turned and saw an elderly gentleman smiling at me. He looked as though he was in his seventies. He had a hearing aid with wire coming out his shirt.

"The Open?" I had no idea what he was talking about.

He walked over and extended his hand. "Hi, my name is Art."

"Carl," I replied, "nice to meet you."

"How long have you been playing?"

I paused wondering how to answer. "Not long."

"First time?"

"Yes," I smiled.

"It shows."

"Oh yeah, where?"

"Want to hit a few?"

Hit a few? I thought. This guy looks as though he could barely walk.

"It's okay, I'll go easy on you," he prompted.

How could I say no with that confidence? Anyway, everyone else had already rejected me.

"Sure," I replied. We walked to Court 21, the court farthest from the action.

With the dedication of a father and the patience of Job, he began the lesson. I didn't realize how hard the game was to play well. I was awful. I swung the racket like a baseball bat. By the end of an hour, I at least knew how to stroke the ball. I couldn't do it well, but I understood how. Finally, at the end of about two hours, he showed me how to serve. Miraculously, I served the ball perfectly. I had been a pitcher in Little League and the motion was exactly the same. One after another, I whacked the serve perfectly. I think that really impressed him.

He then abruptly stopped and walked away. He turned at the gate and said, "Come back tomorrow, we'll try it again." Emotionless, he turned and disappeared over the hill.

I began to wonder why this guy was helping me. Maybe he was a fag? He was an old man; what could he do, I thought? I showed up the next day and the next. From late May to late August, seven days a week, I met Art at 3 PM for two hours a day.

Little by little, I improved. By August, we were playing doubles on the tenth court. My serve became a rocket, and my ground stroke became more and more consistent.

Art was a machine. He stood at the baseline and kept me running constantly. He rarely moved more than a few feet. He was also rude, especially when I made an unforced error.

"Pay attention! Focus! Get that racket back sooner! Get off your heels!" Many times he'd get so mad he'd just leave. "I quit, I'm wasting my time," he'd say. He always came back the next day.

Each week we moved steadily toward Court 1.

In early September, instead of just walking away, he sat me down and informed me that on Saturday we were scheduled to play Jack and Felix. Jack and Felix were the best doubles players on the courts. In their early sixties, they were like machines—a couple of guys who loved the game and had been playing all their lives.

"Okay," I said nonchalantly. It was then I found out how intense Art was about this match.

Grabbing me by the chin, he said, "Look at me, this is very important. You owe me. Don't fuck up." I got the message.

Saturday, the match started promptly at 9 AM. We held our own the first set but ended up losing 7–5. I thought Art was going to have a heart attack. Every time, I missed a shot he'd make a noise.

I loosened up the second and third set. My serve couldn't have been better. We won the second 6–4 and the third 6–2. Art was ecstatic.

I walked over to the bench to rest and collect my things. I was feeling great.

Out of the corner of my eye, I saw Jack hand Art a stack of bills. Art put the bills in his tennis bag.

He walked over to me, shook my hand, and congratulated me on a great match.

"What's with dough?" I asked.

"Oh, you saw that?"

"Yes."

"Well, I bet Jack and Felix a thousand bucks back in May that I could find a novice, train him, and beat them in doubles by September. Luckily, you came along."

"Pretty risky bet," I said.

"I made it after I saw you serve that first day. You don't think that I spent all that time with you because I liked you? What do I look like…a fag?"

"I *was* wondering. By the way, what's my cut?"

"Close your eyes. What do you see? If I deduct for the lessons, you owe me a grand!"

"What if we lost?" I asked.

"Nothing personal, but I would have killed you."

Laughing, Art disappeared over the hill. About a month later, he died in his sleep. I miss him. I owe him big time, regardless of his motives.

Back at breakfast in Acapulco, I asked Manuel if there were any tennis courts nearby.

"How well do you play?" he asked.

"I'm an A club player," I said, "but I just want to hit a few."

"Give me ten minutes." Manuel disappeared into his office. A few minutes passed and he reappeared. "How does 1 PM today sound?"

"Great!"

"I got you an hour with Armando, the pro at Las Brisas. It's a five-minute cab ride right up on the hill behind us."

Las Brisas was a beautiful property. It had individual cottages tucked into the side of the mountain overlooking the bay with private pools.

The main building had a large pool, restaurant, and tennis court. The main pool had a bar built into the side with the stools in the water.

I tracked down Armando at the restaurant. He was a tall Italian from Argentina. The hotel had a single clay court with an adjacent cabana. We started to rally with a nice relaxed pace. The afternoon Acapulco sun was really hot and I could feel it radiating off the top of my head. In fact, Armando suggested that I get a hat. Stupidly, I refused.

About fifteen minutes into our warmup, I suggested that we play a game. The pace picked up, but I was holding my own. The score was 3 to 5 when I began my serve. I hit my first serve wide but it nicked the service line just out Armando's reach. Armando applauded the ace.

Like a scene from a Sam Peckinpaw movie, suddenly everything went into slow motion. I threw the ball up over my head and pulled back on my racket. Just as I was about to follow through, the world went black. I felt a floating, euphoric sensation, then the powdered taste of dirt. I had collapsed from the sun in the middle of my serve.

They dragged me out of the sun over to the cabana. I could suddenly hear someone say, "The poor guy dropped like a brick. I told him to wear a hat."

As I opened my eyes, I could feel the cold, wet facecloth draped over my forehead and eyes. I removed the cloth and saw her beautiful green eyes. It was Lisa, the girl that I met at the El Presidente pool bar the day before.

"How do you feel?" she said, placing another cold cloth on my face.

"Embarrassed," I pulled the cloth off my face. "Aren't you the girl?"

"Yes, Lisa. Carlo, right?"

"Right." I was excited that she remembered me.

"My brother told you to wear a hat. You should have listened. The Acapulco sun is very powerful."

"Your brother is Armando?"

After an hour of cooling down and my drinking lots of liquids, we headed for the pool bar. Armando had accepted a guest pro job offer at the hotel for a couple of months. Lisa and some of Armando's friends were visiting from Argentina. There were five rich guys and five rich girls who partied for a living. They called themselves *The Sacred Family*.

I got along with the group immediately. They couldn't understand why I was traveling alone. They called me the orphan and after a few drinks, they decided to adopt me. I think not only because they liked Americans, but also because I was Italian. From that moment on, I couldn't pay for anything. Lisa and I became an item and I ended up in her suite for the rest of the week. In fact, I only used my room at the El Presidente to store my luggage. It was exciting, romantic, and from what I can remember, fun.

We drove around town in the Jeeps from Las Brisas. Acapulco is loaded with nightclubs and discos. They were wired all over town. We never waited in lines but were ushered in the side doors. We drank margaritas and cases of Dom Perignon champagne.

One night we went to La Quebrada to watch the divers. The famous cliffs rose over 100 feet above the ocean. The divers climbed up the cliff to a shrine, said a prayer, waited for the waves to surge in, and over they went. The El Mirador hotel was built into the cliffs. Most people watched from the hotel balcony.

The "family" decided to get a closer look. We climbed down the cliff opposite the divers. We sat on a ledge that jutted out about 30 feet above the water. We were cheering the divers on when Jaime slipped and fell into the ocean. The old saying that God watches out for the drunks is true. He landed just as the surge hit. Within seconds, a dozen divers were in the water saving him. I was shocked. They thought it was funny.

We went parasailing and water skiing during the day and drank and ate all night. The week ended as quickly as it started. The last night with Lisa was wonderful. Her room overlooked the bay and the full moon shown directly through the sliding door. We didn't sleep a wink. I can still see the sheer white drapes dancing in the light breeze and the moon reflecting off the marble. Her tanned body looked like a piece of sweet chocolate resting on the white sheets.

I was surprised at how well I handled the situation. I was impressionable, young, and naive. I was surprised that I didn't fall hopelessly in love and make an ass of myself.

I was trying to be cool. It, to this day, still feels like a dream.

The next morning Lisa and a few of the family drove me to the airport. Before boarding, I kissed Lisa good-bye and said, "Lisa, I'll never forget you." It sounded corny, but seemed so appropriate.

She smiled warmly, and simply said, "I know."

31

Off to Bean Town

With all the hustling I did in high school and college, I graduated with a few thousand dollars in the bank. After I left the insurance job, I needed a car. Pontiac had just come out with a new sports car called the Firebird. I still remember as if it just happened yesterday. I walked into the Pontiac showroom and there on the floor was a new 1967, olive green Firebird 400 with a white convertible top and white faux leather interior. It had the outlandish sticker price of $3,450.00. I wrote a check on the spot and drove it home. To this day, I still feel a special excitement when I bring home a new car.

Now, nine months later, I was packing up for my move to Boston. I just returned from Acapulco and was filled with adventure. Since I didn't own anything, packing was easy. A couple of suitcases full of clothes, an old radio, and an iron my mother packed so that I could keep my clothes pressed. I hugged my folks and headed for Boston. Little did I know, at the time, that I would never return to Albany to live.

Boston was about a three-hour drive. I arrived late Sunday afternoon, and checked into the Copley Plaza Hotel. American gave me about a month to find a place to live so I thought I'd live comfortably in the meantime. The office was about a mile away on Federal Street near South Station.

I reported the next morning for work. There were six salesmen covering the greater Boston area, a sales manager, and a director of sales. This is a large staff by today's standards to perform a relatively simple task, but it was the late sixties, before computers, fax machines, and cell phones. Large sales offices were common.

My territory was confined to Boston proper where I was assigned about thirty corporations and about twenty travel agencies. I called on insurance and financial companies, some law offices, and my biggest account, Gillette Razor.

There isn't much pressure in a regulated industry so everyone was helpful and happy. In fact, the reason getting a salesman's job at an airline was so hard was that no one ever left. The average seniority was fifteen years. In order to get fired, you needed to commit a crime or do something immoral like harass a customer. Of course, at that time, *harassment* was hardly defined.

My job consisted of convincing the customers to use American over the other airlines. Since the fares and schedules were all regulated, all I could do was pass out brochures, listen to complaints, promote new in-flight services, and be charming. As long as I was a good soldier, I would have an ulcer-free job for life. Unfortunately, that was improbable.

The next weekend I started looking for a place to live. Someone mentioned that living by the shore would be a good idea. I took that advice and found a small apartment in Marblehead, the famous fishing and sailing town located about twenty miles north of Boston.

The summer was great fun. The weather was perfect and days long. I found the local pub, Mattie's Sail Loft, and quickly made friends.

The lobster fishermen were great guys. They worked long hours in the worst weather but had a great attitude. We drank up a storm the night before, and still they got up at 4 AM the next morning for work. I also made friends with the guys who owned the compass company—the three Baker Brothers. They invited me to crew with them. The first few trips were a disaster. I knew nothing about sailing. They'd yell out, "Grab the line," and I'd yell back, "Where, which one, what's a line?" I learned the language just in time to realize that I hated sailing. Incidentally, *crew* is a euphemism for slave worker. It was too much work for not going anywhere. Also, throwing up regularly was not my idea of a fun afternoon.

By September, Marblehead had lost its charm. The drive to Boston each morning was a drag. The fall was overcast and cold, and the town emptied out of tourists. Even the bars closed before midnight. It was time to get out.

I became friendly with one of my travel agents, Bill Hokkenen. He was looking for a roommate. I had never lived with anyone but my family so this would be a new experience. Bill was living in a new apartment building overlooking the Charles River on Commonwealth in Kenmore Square. It was a great building, great location, but only had one bedroom.

Hokkenen's solution was to build one. To this day, I'm not sure what possessed me to go along with this lunacy. The next day I arrived home and the closet in the kitchen had been removed and a room in the living room had been framed. We lived in the state of construction for almost a year. He was always broke and never completed the project. Thank God my name wasn't on the lease.

Bill was always figuring and occasionally came up with a good idea. He worked with an English guy named Bobby Sheldon. Bobby was recently separated. His wife had returned to England and he was stuck with a big duplex in Beacon Hill. His friend, also from England, was a visiting professor at Harvard. He was going somewhere in the Middle East for a year for an archeological dig and wanted to rent out his furnished house in Framingham.

Follow this logic. We joined forces financially. We rented the upper floor of the duplex on Beacon Hill to three stewardesses for $320 per month, or $20 per month more than the entire apartment rental. We rented the house from his friend for $275 per month. The apartment in Kenmore Square cost $225 per month. For $160 per month per person, we had three places to live.

The house in Framingham was on the Sudbury River Reservoir and had a waterfall in the yard. At the time, it all seemed very cool—not practical but cool. We'd pick up girls with the line, "Would you like to go to my place on Beacon Hill? Maybe something livelier in Kenmore Square, or would you prefer to see my waterfall in Framingham?" This was Bill's solution to appeasing me for the Kenmore Square insanity. This arrangement lost its luster when I started dating my future wife and spent most of my time at her place.

Prior to my moving to Boston, I saw a picture of American's representative in the Miss Interline contest in Las Vegas in the company newspaper, the *AstroJet News*. She was a beautiful, shapely blonde with long legs and a small, Bridget Bardot-looking face. I remember feeling a connection to the picture. I forgot about her until months later when I was walking through the Boston office and I saw this shapely blonde walking toward me. She was more beautiful in person, and her presence stopped me in my tracks.

"Excuse me, aren't you that girl who was in the *Astrojet News*?" I asked awkwardly.

"Yes, a couple of times," she said with a smile.

"I'm Carl, I'm the new sales rep."

"Robin," she said extending her hand.

"You're very good looking—good enough to eat." I couldn't believe what just slipped out. *What a stupid thing to say,* I thought.

She chuckled and started to walk away. After a few steps, she turned. "I'll take that as a compliment." Laughing, she disappeared into the cafeteria.

Now, that's one cool lady, I thought. I finally mustered the nerve to ask her out. On our first date, we went to the combat zone in downtown Boston and found a great blues bar. The conversation was smooth and the evening couldn't have been more fun. When we got home, I respectfully kissed her good night.

"I had a great time," I said.

"Me, too."

"Can I see you again?"

"No!" She said it so casually. It shocked me.

"Did you say no?"

"Yes, no!"

"Can I ask why?"

"You're too young."

"We're the same age."

"Exactly, I prefer older men."

"How about if I grew a mustache and a pot belly?"

"Good night." She threw me a kiss and closed the door.

Rejected! No one's ever rejected me before. *This means war,* I thought. As it turned out, I persisted, and we secretly dated the entire time I was in Boston. A year later, we were married and we're still together after thirty-five years.

Meanwhile, back at the office, American Airlines was getting into the hotel business. I took a group of travel agents on a "fam" to Dallas, and we decided to stay at one of American's New Flagship Hotels: The Inn of the Six Flags. The trip was a disaster. The hotel didn't have our reservation, we had to stay somewhere else for a night, and dinner arrangements were screwed up. It was a mess.

When I returned home, I sent a fiery letter to the head of the hotel division. The letter could have been more tactful and I could have copied my superiors. Again, I did the right thing only in the wrong way.

The letter went bouncing around the management in Boston. The hotel division was sensitive of their relationship to the airline and the last thing they needed was airline personnel badmouthing the fledgling hotel company.

After I was dressed down for sending a letter to the corporate office without permission, I was told that the hotel's vice president of marketing in New York wanted to see me. I flew to New York the next day and met with a group of hotel executives. I do write excellent complaint letters! Instead of being hammered, they offered me a job. I was to be the Manager of Airline Sales and responsible for promoting the hotel with the airline personnel.

I had to move to New York and my salary was bumped to $15,000. *This is fun,* I thought: two years, three promotions, and twice the salary. Now in addition to free airline travel, I got free hotel rooms plus free rein to meet anyone I wanted to in the company.

I moved to New York two weeks later, and moved in with Pete "Greenjeans" Greenfield.

Pete worked for American in the home office as the manager of cabin services. He had a great two-bedroom apartment on 74th Street off Second on the fashionable East Side of New York.

I was now in the hotel business and had never worked a day in a hotel. Well, this ought to be interesting.

32

I Put Them Between the Sheets

If you're not from a big city, New York is a scary place. Even though Boston had introduced me to city living, New York was still intimidating. I saw the ad for a roommate on the company bulletin board the day I interviewed. I called Mr. Pete Greenfield and told him about my move. We arranged to have lunch the day I started my job in New York.

"Greenjeans," as I nicknamed him, was an Ivy-League type with an MBA from Princeton. He was a little stiff but seemed like a straightforward, friendly guy. Although he lacked a cool gene, I could see that he was ready to have a good time. I liked him and I saw that we could get along. He mentioned that he traveled about 40 percent of the time in his role as manager of cabin services.

He explained that he reported to the vice president of marketing and that his job was to help ensure the quality of the service that a passenger experienced once on board the flight. This involved food and beverages, movies, stewardesses, etc. The double benefit of befriending Pete was that he knew his way around the corporate office. This was important because, in my new capacity, I needed to develop relationships with the department heads.

We made the deal and I moved into the large two-bedroom the next day. It was a great apartment on the corner off 74th Street and Second Avenue. I rented a bed and dresser and I was settled.

In spite of his corporate, buttoned-down manner, Pete deep down wanted to be a player. He was like the person who tells a joke and flubs the punch line. He was almost there.

He had some connection with the stewardess college in Texas, because every couple of weeks, three or four stewardesses would stay at the apartment for a few days while they were searching for a place to live. Pete was gone half the time so I was there to make sure they were comfortable, very comfortable.

American's hotel expansion started immediately. Within a few months, they opened properties in Seoul, Honolulu, Mexico City Acapulco, and Fiji. Within a month of starting work, I was sent to Korea to help open the Chosun Hotel.

The trip to Korea was an oppressive thirteen hours. You lost or gained a day depending on which direction you were flying, and the fuel stop in Alaska didn't help much. Jon Day and I were sent to oversee the pre-opening and to represent the airline in the day-to-day decision-making. Jon was the new director of food and beverage. He was British educated and recently moved from Chile.

Jon was a welcome companion not only because I liked his dry iconoclastic wit, but because he had years of hotel experience, which I so desperately needed to tap. As it turned out, my four weeks with him was a remarkable experience. He was extremely generous in sharing his knowledge and patient in teaching me the ropes. No school could have duplicated the quality of this knowledge transfer. I was very lucky to have found such a mentor.

The only negative was that Jon was irritated that the company had sent him away so soon after his marriage. He was thirty-five and this was his third wife, so his protests were a little suspect. In fact, his protests abruptly ended when he saw how many beautiful available Korean women were milling around the new hotel.

The Chosen was the first true luxury hotel in Korea. Located right in the heart of Seoul, the hotel's modern architecture really made an impression on us as we were landing.

Jon moved us into the presidential suite, a decadent 2000-square-foot house located on the 20th floor. It had a private elevator, three bedrooms, a magnificent living room with a nine-foot Steinway, and a formal dining room with a table that sat fourteen. His logic was that since we were working twenty-four hours a day, seven days a week, the least we should expect was a little comfort. How could I argue with such brilliance?

Opening a hotel, especially an international one, was a Herculean task. The logistics were mind-boggling. The rooms had to be furnished and the maids trained. The signs in the public areas and the literature in every room had to be correct in several languages. Menus had to be designed and food and beverage staff trained as must valet parkers, front office personnel, security—the list seemed endless. Luckily, the hotel had hired an outstanding international staff. The GM was from Germany and the food and beverage manager was from Italy, both seasoned veterans who had opened hotels all over the world. Jon was kind enough to keep my inexperience hidden, and I worked hard at playing the role of the serious corporate manager. I nodded and smiled until I was comfortable with the language of hotel management and the problems needing resolution. I understood the excitement that the "great imposter" must have felt.

Our typical day consisted of getting up at 7 AM and having a champagne breakfast in the formal dining room. I think we drank most of the Dom Perignon in the hotel. We worked until five and then went to the Chin-Chin Hotel for a massage.

The massage was 900 *won* or $3 dollars. It was 1800 *won* for a massage with a happy ending. In Asia, the massage is a ritual. First, you're put in a steam cabinet to clean out your pores. Next, you're sat on a stool and scrubbed with a large, rough sponge to clean the skin and to remove the dead tissue. Then, warm water is poured over you to wash away any debris. Finally, you're soaked in a big tub, dried off, and given a deep tissue massage. It was wonderfully relaxing.

After the massage, we returned to the hotel, worked until nine, and then we had dinner. After dinner, we'd drink or drive over to Walker Hill to gamble. The only problem was that we had to leave before midnight and couldn't return until 4 AM. The South Koreans had a curfew designed to prevent infiltration from the north. Since we had so much political juice, sometime we'd run the stockades.

One night, we each won over $1500 at the blackjack table. At that time, you couldn't exchange *won* back to greenbacks even if you started with U.S. dollars. They wanted you to keep the *won* and spend it before you left the country. We each carried 500,000 *won* stuffed in our pockets and in our shirts. It looked as though we had just robbed a bank. That night we left early and, as a result, we were stopped at each checkpoint. By the time we got home, we had each paid out about 100,000 *won* in bribes. When at two in the morning, someone sticks a machine gun in the window, giving a little peace offering seems like a small sacrifice.

The rest of the month went smoothly. The opening was a smashing success with diplomats from several countries attending. We did enjoy one fringe benefit. The opening called for a fashion show. A dozen of Korea's most beautiful models participated. Of course, during the several rehearsals we felt obligated to entertain them in our presidential suite. *The details will be covered in the uncensored edition.*

With a major opening under my belt, I was feeling very cocky. One would think that I had spent as much time as Eloise did at the Plaza. Jon flew home, and I was sent to Suva, Fiji to oversee the Flagship

Beachcomber opening. It was a small property and should have been a simple assignment.

I arrived a week before the opening and met Jeremy, the GM. He was a likable young guy from New Zealand. The hotel was in great shape so I was looking forward to a week on the beach. Two days before the opening, we were having a drink by the pool when the front office manager came running up and announced that one of the maids was having a seizure. When we got to the room, the woman was calm but Harold, the local representative, explained that the hotel was possessed with evil spirits. Harold wasn't a union guy but kind of a business agent for the local workers.

"Possessed! Harold, You've got to be kidding."

"Sorry, but they won't work unless it's exorcized."

I looked at Jeremy, "Shall we call a priest?"

"I think we need a witch doctor," Jeremy said with a smile.

"Do you have one?" I asked. "The opening is in forty-eight hours."

"I know a guy, guaranteed." Harold interrupted.

"How much?" I asked.

"I can probably get him…if he's available…on such short notice for…$800."

"$800," we yelled back in unison.

"When's the opening?"

"Good point, bring him in!"

The next morning we waited outside the front entrance for our evil spirit exterminator. A jeep pulled up and out came a Fijian-looking gentleman, stocky, shoulder-length hair, wearing a polo shirt, and Gucci loafers.

With a big smile, he extended his hand and in a slight British accent he said, "Good morning, my name is Bing. Harold said you needed help…the hotel is stunning."

"Bing, your name is Bing?" I blurted out.

"Yes, my mother loved those Crosby and Hope road movies."

I looked at Jeremy in despair. "Are you sure you want to do this?"

"If you cosign the rec, I'll be your friend forever. Unless you have a better idea."

"How about $500?"

"My price is $800. If I knew a big American corporation was involved, it would have been $2500. I'm giving you a deal because Harold and I are chums."

"Okay, deal. Do you guarantee results?"

"...For the life of the hotel, or if someone else buys it, whichever comes first. Cash, right!"

"Right, what do you need?"

"I'm fine, I've brought everything. Where can I change?"

We took him to the room where the maid had flipped out. He went into the bathroom, and ten minutes later he appeared in full witch doctor regalia.

He was a changed man—no British accent, no Gucci loafers. His painted face and feathered headdress exaggerated the wild look in his eyes. He danced around, yelled, threw exploding powder. It was a real show. We had the entire local staff in attendance to witness the exorcism. Finally, he screamed and fainted. It was a good show. Not worth eight hundred but at least he scared the shit out of some of the help.

After a few minutes he got up, walked back into the room and changed back into his street clothes. Jeremy handed him the envelope with the money.

As we walked him back to the car, he turned and asked, "Your bar isn't open, by any chance, is it? I could use a martini."

"Not until Friday. But if you come back this weekend, dinner and martinis are on the house."

I figured we needed this guy on our side. He thanked me, wished us luck, and said he'd be back Saturday with his girlfriend.

The hotel opening went smoothly, and Sunday morning I was back on a plane headed for home.

Before the end the year, we opened hotels in Hawaii, Mexico City, and Acapulco. In the middle of this excitement, I got married and started a family.

In the next two years, the company acquired the Americana Hotels from Loews Corporation. By 1974, the Americana Hotels managed over twenty upscale hotel properties in the U.S., Caribbean, Hawaii, and the Far East and South Pacific. I had been promoted several times and, by the age of thirty, I was vice president of marketing.

It was exciting, educational, and now I was bored.

33

Park Avenue Penthouse

The Health Roof Club was a little-known gym located on the top floor of an office/warehouse building on 45th Street just east of Second Avenue. I don't remember how I found it but it wasn't expensive, had good equipment and an impressive membership. Forty-fifth Street east of Second had an aging quality to it. There wasn't much there but pre-war office buildings and old apartments. The gym had been around for years and showed its age. Health clubs hadn't evolved to the social high-tech meeting grounds that they are today. They were still called gyms, and only the most advanced had the first-generation Nautilus equipment.

The equipment was adequate with free weights and some pulleys. The real attraction was that it had two handball/racquetball courts and one squash court. I learned to play squash in Albany from the same old guys with whom I played tennis in the summer. Little did I know at the time that squash was such an elitist sport and that it would eventually help define social status.

The membership was principally Jewish. They were mostly entrepreneurs who owned their businesses, with a few advertising executives and entertainment people in the mix. David Susskind, the TV talk show host of the seventies; Vidal Sassoon, the hair guy; and Ed Ney, the chairman of Young and Rubican, were examples of the quality of the membership. There was a large steam and sauna where everyone socialized after their workout. It was very easy to make friends, especially since I was one of the better squash/racquetball players and played regularly. Within six months, I was on a first-name basis with most of the regulars. I loved talking to the old Jewish businessmen. They had a perfect mixture of paranoia and wisdom.

I was the director of sales programs at the time for Americana, so I was constantly being told about their vacation deals and about their airline horror stories. It was all very friendly.

One of the members was Henry Golightly. Henry ran an international management consultant firm. He grew up in Texas and eventually worked for McKenzie and Associates, the world-renowned consulting firm. It was there that Henry made his many high-level corporate contacts. He went out on his own and acquired some high-profile clients including American, Continental, Braniff, and PanAm Airlines; Norton Simon, Inc.; and a number of advertising agencies. He focused on senior-level management reorganizations and executive recruiting. He was very successful. Truman Capote rented his gatehouse in Bridgehampton one year where he wrote *Breakfast at Tiffany's* and named the main character, Holly Golightly, after Henry.

I saw him regularly in the steam room and often we talked about the airline business. Before long, we became friends. Thirty years my senior, with tons of management experience and contacts, he was the mentor that I needed.

I had been vice president of marketing for more than a year when Henry mentioned a search he was conducting. The chairman/president of Norton Simon, Inc. was looking for an assistant. Henry was conducting the search and asked if I wanted to interview. I told him that I didn't know the company or the chairman and had no idea what an assistant to the chairman/president did.

Henry, in his wisdom, guided me through my stupidity. NSI was an international consumer product company. The chairman, David

Mahoney, was one of the premier chief executives in the country, and the job would be a learning experience equal to a Harvard Business School degree.

Meanwhile, back at the office, the hotel company was growing at the speed of light. In my four years the company had grown to over twenty hotels. We acquired the Americanas in New York, Florida, and Puerto Rico, along with their senior management at the Loews Corporation. The Americanas were large convention hotels as opposed to the business traveler/resort hotels of Flagship.

Jim Himbaugh and his management team from Loews were tough street fighters who were tightly wired to the unions. Their arrival caused a real cultural conflict. I was the last of the old flagship team. The rest had either found other jobs or were let go. I not only survived but also had absorbed other responsibilities. I was the go-to person when something needed to be found, or had to be done. I ran the advertising, tours, and joint programs with the airlines and wrote the presentations to the board. While no one was looking, I was securing my future. The VP job was given to me, as much in recognition for what I controlled as it was a tribute to my talent. In fact, the new management was a little uncomfortable with my presence, but we tried to get along.

The hotel chairman, Carter Burgess, could never figure out how I moved up so quickly. At thirty, I was probably the youngest VP in the company. Burgess, who was one of great old-boy stories, had been a chairman with TWA as well as on the board of a number of Fortune 500 companies.

With his old Virginia accent, bushy eyebrows, and portly figure, he was a cross between "Foghorn Leghorn" and Colonel Sanders. He had two offices: one large corner office that he used as a personal conference room and a small outer office where he sat in the corner at his roll-top desk with his overhead ceiling fan and held his one-on-one meetings.

He loved to mispronounce my name and take jabs at me like, "If I could buy you for what you're worth, son, and sell you for what you think you're worth, I could retire."

When all things were considered, with the most important being that my learning curve had flattened out, the timing for my finding a new challenge seemed right. I agreed to the Norton Simon interview. The offices at AA were Spartan with cubicles and a few selected offices. The furniture was basic and the artwork consisted of airline destination posters. Norton Simon headquarters, on the other hand, screamed of opulence and good taste. They occupied the 45th and 46th floor of the Chemical Bank building at 277 Park Avenue, two blocks south of the Waldorf Astoria Hotel—a most prestigious address.

Dressed in my black Pierre Cardin, I took a deep breath and entered the elevator. After a nosebleed forty-five-floor ride, the door opened to plush, monochromatic gray carpet and fabric-covered walls. The reception area consisted of a large wood and brass structure that looked more like a small boat than a desk, where two well-dressed, attractive women sat taking calls and greeting guests. A guard stood unobtrusively in the corner.

"May I help you?" one of the women asked.

"I have a two o'clock appointment with Mr. Mahoney."

"Your name?"

"Cusato, Carl Cusato."

She picked up the phone and announced my arrival.

"Please take a seat. Someone will be out shortly. Would you like some coffee or a cold drink?"

I sat down and absorbed my surroundings. The large modern paintings and high ceilings made me feel more like I was in a museum. I picked up the annual report and saw a picture of Mahoney. He was a handsome guy in his late 40s, early 50s with eyes so focused they looked as if they were bulging out of his head. In my research, I learned that NSI had been formed in 1968, when the industrialist and art collector Norton Simon decided to consolidate his investments into one international customer products company. They owned Hunt Foods; Canada Dry; Somerset Importers, a liquor company which distributed Johnny Walker, Tanqueray Gin, Old Fitzgerald Bourbon, and a variety of other distilled products; Max Factor Cosmetics; *McCalls* and *Redbook* magazines; McCall Patterns; a glass and can company; and a chemical company. It was one of the earlier conglomerates.

Suddenly, a woman's voice with a British accent interrupted my reading.

"Mr. Cusato?"

Looking up, I saw a pretty young woman in a tailored suit with an elegant silk blouse.

"Yes."

"I'm Barbara, Mr. Mahoney's assistant. Follow me."

She led me down a long corridor with large works of art hanging from the walls. At the end of the corridor were two large brass-textured doors that led into an outer sitting room. Through the sitting room was the secretarial area where Barbara and her assistant sat. The office complex must have been 3000 square feet. She led me into Mahoney's sitting room, which looked like a library and had unobstructed views of the city.

As I sat there waiting, I wondered whether I was interviewing for a job or waiting to see the Wizard of Oz. From what I had read, Mahoney was a true American dream story. He grew up in the Bronx to a lower-middle-class Irish family. He started as an account guy with an advertising agency and eventually opened his own agency. He became a senior market executive with Proctor and Gamble and next president of Good Humor Ice Cream. Norton Simon hired him to be president of

Canada Dry. When NSI was formed, he was named president but ran the company with two other executives. Eventually the troika didn't work out, and he was named President and Chairman.

As Mahoney entered the room, I could feel his charisma.

"Hi, I'm David." I stood as he extended his hand. "Please sit down."

As I sat, I thought, *what a powerful presence this guy has.*

"Henry tells me you're a very bright young man. Are you?"

"I'm not sure what 'bright' means anymore." Trying to settle my nervousness.

"Really, why do you say that?"

"I know bright people who regularly make terrible decisions. Now if you said 'street smart,' I'd be more comfortable with the compliment."

"Well said. Tell me a little about yourself."

I did about a two-minute recap, trying to appeal to his entrepreneurial spirit.

When I finished, he shook his head and said that he had one more guy to interview—a Harvard man. When I heard that, I felt my chances disappearing.

"Before you go, let me tell you a little about the position," he said.

"As my assistant, you'll be dealing with princes and paupers. You will work long hours and I expect for you to ensure that I am never surprised. Unfortunately, you will be asked for non-business help as well as the normal business issues. Our relationship is seamless in that way. When we travel, Barbara will handle the details but you will be responsible for it to go smoothly. Most importantly, I need someone that I can trust. Violate my trust and it will be over immediately—no second chances. I need someone with good judgment. You will have access to sensitive information that people will constantly be trying to get from you. You must know what to say and what not to say. I need someone with good instincts. This is not an easy job but the rewards can be substantial if you're smart. We'll be in touch. It was nice meeting you." Pressing the intercom, "Barbara! Barbara will show you out."

I walked out not really sure how well I had done. It sounded very exciting, but also a little scary. My financial skills weren't that great at the time, and I was worried about my ability to do the analysis part.

Two days later, I received a call from Barbara to come back. *Good sign,* I thought.

This time, I was escorted into his office and sat at his desk. He hung up the phone and said, "The job is yours if you want it."

"Great!" I said.

"How does $32,000 plus benefits and stock options sound?"

I made a face.

"Something wrong?"

"It's a little thin." I held my breath. "I was hoping for thirty-five."

"Okay, if thirty-five makes you happy. You got it."

I began to wonder if I'd sold myself too cheaply. His response was too quick.

"And a review in six months," I countered.

He started to laugh. "Don't worry, in this job you're reviewed daily!"

In the two weeks before starting the job, I read every book on finance that I could find. I also read and re-read the company's annual reports for the previous five years. My friends at American were happy for me. Even Burgess made a point to come to my office and wish me luck. His comment was, "...So I hear you're leaving us to sell ketchup. Good luck."

My NSI office was located next to Mahoney's main office. It was large, about 20 by 15, with a couch, two chairs, a coffee table, and a pair of original Ellsworth Kelly paintings on the wall. My large picture windows looked south on Park Avenue. I asked for coffee, and a tray with a silver carafe, two cups of milk and sugar were delivered. If only the Second Avenue boys could see me now.

I spent this first week meeting the senior executives. Since nothing was made or sold at the corporate office, the executive staff consisted of financial analysts, lawyers, and strategic planners. These were smart, aggressive people. The business magazines had named Mahoney Fortune 500's toughest executive. Since I was to have his ear, everyone was interested in knowing what kind of person he would be dealing with. I realized that I quickly needed to develop not only the right business skills but also the right interpersonal skills to deal with these guys. I had no idea how much power my position carried in the company, not only with the executive staff but also with the operating company presidents. Even though I was only an "assistant to," I had the boss's ear and that was valuable.

I approached the job as I did most things in my life: I sat back and learned as I went along. My first lesson was that less is more. The less that I said about myself or about my opinion on a matter, the stronger I appeared. I had to be careful. This was a shark factory.

The boardroom, where the Directors met, and where we held the staff and subsidiary company operating reviews, was a study in Machiavellian behavior. A 25-foot, polished mahogany table, shaped like a flattened pyramid, and more than a dozen plush, upholstered swivel chairs filled the room. At the top of the pyramid was space for two chairs: one for the chairman and one for me. Along the slope of the table sat the senior corporate executives in order of rank. On the flat side of the table sat the senior execs of the company or department being reviewed. The senior staff would meet at least weekly while the operating company inquisitions were held quarterly. It was all about making the numbers and ensuring the success of the stock price.

As I look back, I realize that my greatest strength was that I was too naive to get the magnitude and complexity of my surroundings. I was just a regular, uncomplicated guy sitting in the middle of a shark tank. I think Mahoney saw this as a comforting quality in me. I never tried to compete with the staff and never used my power for personal gain. If I knew then what I know now, it may have been more of a problem than a benefit.

I am not saying that I didn't "fuck" with people's heads from time to time, only that I never used it as a weapon.

My job was to ensure that the chairman was prepared. I would collect the subject analysis before each meeting and go over it with him in detail. I tried to be an additional set of eyes and ears. My greatest strength was that I never gave anyone a reason *not* to trust me. I was always up front, as much as I could be, on what I could do or not do. With such high-power competitors, there was always intrigue, insecurity, and subtle back-stabbing. Mahoney was a master at manipulating the weaknesses of this environment. Information was the weapon. The best way to make a powerful corporate executive crazy is to take him out of the information loop.

The fun part of the job was that I was responsible for the corporate jet, the limos, and the apartment in the Waldorf Towers. We had a two-engine British Aircraft Corp 111, named the "Skyrunner," that seated twenty-two. We never flew twenty-two. The average load was five or six. It had a bedroom, a lounge, and a full galley.

Once a year, we'd schedule an investor relations trip to Europe. The limo would take us from the office on 47th Street to the 60th Street heliport where a helicopter took us to Teterboro Airport in New Jersey. There, "Skyrunner" sat awaiting our arrival. Our crew of two pilots and a flight attendant greeted us at the ramp, loaded our luggage, and it was "wheels up."

Our first stop was St. John's, Newfoundland for fuel. From there, we flew directly to Luton Airport in the UK. At Luton, we boarded two jet ranger helicopters, one for the people, one for the luggage. We then flew to the Butterick Park heliport in London where a Phantom Six Rolls Royce took us to the Claridges Hotel. After a few days in London, it was off to Paris where Jean Claude, our limo driver, met us for the drive to our suites at The Plaza Athenea Hotel. It was not easy to go back to meatballs and spaghetti after all this.

After I unpacked on my first trip to London, I went to Mahoney's room to find out if he needed anything. He told me to dismiss the driver because his dinner companion was picking him up. Instead, I dressed and took the limo on a sightseeing trip through London. Eric, the driver, was so formal that he would only call me Sir. It felt terrific tooting though London while people strained to see who was inside.

After a few hours, Eric suggested a membership pass to The Park Lane casino. In those days, one needed a membership to gamble. He talked to the doorman and my membership magically appeared. Not realizing that I was playing with pounds rather dollars, I was surprised when I won almost $2000 playing blackjack. It happened in less than an hour. I was so shocked, I took the money and ran. It was midnight, and I had no one to tell. I gave Eric 100 pounds and took him to dinner. He was so grateful I think he'll be my friend forever. In the limo the next day, Mahoney asked about my evening. I told him it was uneventful. Eric couldn't wipe the smile from his face.

We traveled often to California where Hunt Foods and Max Factor were located. There, we either stayed at the Beverly Hills Hotel where Cottage 5 was reserved or at the Century Plaza Hotel where Suite 1901 awaited.

Thirty-one H was the corporate apartment at the Waldorf Towers. It was an enormous two bedroom with high ceilings, a large marble foyer, a formal dining room that sat twelve, a large living room, and a den. It was supposed to be used for visiting dignitaries but that happened rarely. We used it for parties, a charitable event in which Mahoney was honored, dinner parties, and afternoon trysts for selected executives and friends. Since I held the keys and kept the liquor cabinet full, I accumulated many friends. It was like a scene out of *The Apartment* with Jack Lemmon.

My six years with NSI was a wonderful learning experience. Not only did I see and do things only reserved for the rich, but I got an insider's view of how large corporations really operate. My relationship with Mahoney remained excellent for the entire time. In fact, the only time there was any friction was when he asked me to fix his tennis court in Bridgehampton. He had hired a driveway contractor to build the court. When the project ran into problems, he asked me to take over. He was headed to Europe for a couple of weeks, and he wanted it finished before he returned.

I took the limo out to the house to meet with the contractor. The contractor, in order to ensure drainage, sloped the court. Unfortunately, the slope was about two feet. As a result, it felt like playing uphill. After about an hour, the contractor finally arrived. I ignored his tardiness.

"Hi, I'm Carl. I am Dave's assistant."

"*Basta, basta,* Fornini," he said with a slight accent.

"Doesn't *basta* mean enough in Italian?"

"Yes, I am the youngest of nine children."

Ignoring the obvious. "I need to get this court fixed for Dave."

"There is nothing wrong with it. It has to drain or there will be puddles."

"I agree, but this looks like you built this court on the side of a hill."

"So you say!"

"So I say? Watch this." I put a ball down, and it rolled to the fence. "Well?'

"It has to drain. Mr. Mahoney insisted on drainage. Anyway, the balls won't get in your way when you play."

"Have you ever built a tennis court before?"

"Sure, lots of them." I knew that he was lying but I didn't have time to screw around.

"How much to straighten it out?"

"$10,000!"

"How 'bout five and I won't sue you?"

"Can't do it. I'll lose money on the job. Anyway, it's not my fault."

I was trying to save Dave money. He complained that Mahoney made a big deal over drainage and that the land shifted. It was one bullshit excuse after another. The discussion became heated.

Finally I said, "*Basta! basta*, $7,500, or we go to court, plus we tell everyone in Bridgehampton what an asshole you are." He agreed.

I returned a week later and, sure enough, he brought in stone and sand and built up the court. In the meantime, I found a new surface being used in Europe. It was weatherproofed polyurethane that was installed like tile. It looked great and had small holes in it, which not only allowed for drainage but also allowed for playing in the light rain. It was slick, high-tech stuff and I was proud of my solution. The only problem was, it would take a few weeks to get. They finished the surface, and installed the fence and net poles. The following Saturday morning, I received a telephone call from the boss.

"How are you doing?"

"Great, Dave, welcome home. How was Rome?"

"Tiring, what are you doing?"

"Just hanging out."

"Oh, good. Did you play tennis this morning?"

"Yeah, early, it was really hot."

"Mmm, guess where I am?"

"Bridgehampton?"

"Brilliant. Guess what I am wearing?"

"A dress?" No laughter, oops!

"Funny, guess where I'm standing? And guess what I'm not doing?"

"What's the problem?"

"I am in my tennis clothes, standing on what was supposed to be a finished court, where I am not playing tennis. Unfortunately, my assistant didn't think it was important enough to do me this personal favor."

"Now, Dave, that's not fair. I had trouble with the contractor redoing without a charge. I was trying to save money and…"

"I didn't ask you to save me money. I asked you to get it done."

"I found this great new…"

"If it were *your* court, I'd be playing. Maybe this job was a little over your head."

He hung up. Apparently, he made plans while in Europe for some mixed doubles, thinking the court would be ready. His hostility, I guess, was out of embarrassment. By Wednesday of the next week, he was still ignoring me. It was a trick I saw him use countless times with his senior guys who didn't perform to his satisfaction.

Luckily, I got a call that afternoon that the surface had arrived. I begged the installer to start right away. I promised him an extra thousand if he finished by Friday. I drove out Friday morning as they were putting on the finishing touches. The red, green and white tiles looked great. I hit a few balls with the installer. The surface was easy on the feet and the court almost played like clay. Rather than call Dave, I wrote him a letter telling him of all the benefits of the new find, and how he was the first in the country to have the new surface.

He never said a word to me. On the following Monday, Barbara buzzed me and told me that Dave wanted me in his office. As I walked in, he was on the phone with one of his rich buddies.

"The surface is incredible. It plays like clay. It's easy on the legs and you can play right after it rains…My guy found it in Europe…It's great stuff…about a buck a foot…I stay ahead of the curve because I have talented people working with me…"

He put his hand over the receiver. Speaking to me, "Send a brochure on the tennis surface over to Phil Segal. Barbara will give you the address."

That was the last I heard of the tennis court. His apology was the compliment he made sure that I heard. Things returned to normal.

34

Where Do You Summer?

Robin, the kids, and I were still living in the apartment in Tudor City on the East Side between 41st Street and 43rd when the "Jewish Flood" hit the Health Roof Club. The elderly couple that owned it wanted to retire to Florida. The fire was just bad enough to demolish the club but not the building. I remember feeling a real loss. I used the club nearly every day. It was convenient and I had made many friends there. I needed to find a new place.

P.J. Johnson was one of the first friends I made when I arrived in New York. I worked with his father at American in Boston, and he introduced us. P.J. had been in the city a few years and knew his way around. He was a journalist major at the University of Missouri, and upon graduation, he landed a job with a public relations firm. He had the perfect personality for PR. He loved corporate intrigue, and was fascinated with my job at NSI. He urged me to keep notes so that I could write a book someday.

At lunch one day, while I was moaning about the fire, P.J. suggested that I consider joining one of New York's men's clubs. Men's clubs in New York had a rich heritage. With origins in the late nineteenth century, these restricted social enclaves were created for the City's carriage trade. There were the school-affiliated clubs like the Harvard, Yale, and Princeton clubs, and then there were the business clubs. The New York Athletic Club (NYAC) had the best athletic facilities. In addition to the gym, it had an indoor track and pool. It was an enormous facility on Central Park South.

The Racquet Club on Park Avenue boasted one of the only *Court Tennis* courts in the country. Court Tennis was the precursor to modern tennis. It was originally played in French courtyards using handmade balls. The court today retains the same look with a sloping roof on one wall. Court tennis combines the athleticism of lawn tennis and squash, the strategy of chess, and the subtlety and variety of golf. It is a sport that challenges the mind and body in equal measure. The game is for the rich and is ridiculously complicated. Who else but the French could invent such a pretentious, complicated sport?

The other notable clubs in town were the Union and Union League. The Downtown Athletic Club awarded the "Heisman Trophy" every year. The Harmony was a club created by Jewish businessmen who were restricted from the other men's clubs.

Of all the men's clubs I found, the New York University Club was the most interesting. It was located in an imposing ten-story, Renaissance-revival building located at 54th Street and 5th Avenue. It had large, high-ceiling rooms with oak-paneled walls. There were big high-back chairs for reading and sleeping, an extensive library, two restaurants, a bar, six squash courts, and a health club in the basement reminiscent of the Roman baths. In the lobby, it had the largest working fireplace that I had ever seen. It also had hotel rooms for members wishing to spend the night or for their out-of-town guests.

The problem was not in choosing a club. The problem was getting into a club. These clubs were not overtly restricted, except for women, but they made the admission process so complex that it was easy to control the demographics of the membership. For example, University Club required five letters of recommendation from active members, an interview, and approval by three members of the admissions committee, and, if you were under thirty-five, approval by the younger men's committee.

P.J. got me a copy of the club directory. There wasn't one name that I recognized, and to make matters worse, I didn't see any names that ended in a vowel. Just as I was about to give the idea the heave, Mahoney walked into my office. I must have had a strange look.

"Who died?" he said with a smile and sat down.

"You know, my club burned down."

"Yeah, Henry told me."

"I was hoping to join the University Club, but I don't know any members."

"It's a great club, a little stuffy. They could probably use someone like you to give it color. Give me the book."

He looked over the directory. "I see that Carl Desch is the head of the admissions committee. He's also the Vice Chairman of Citibank. They handle our account. Good guy. I'll call him. Maybe he can help."

Mahoney was an expert at leverage. He had a way of asking for a favor that made you want to say yes. I had an appointment the next day.

Mr. Desch could not have been nicer. He arranged for me to meet five members who agreed to write letters. I also interviewed with the three admissions committee members.

It looked like a slam-dunk until I was invited to the younger men's committee cocktail party. It was being held from 6 to 8 PM in one of the club's function rooms.

I arrived just after six. In the room stood about a dozen committee members and about six candidates. I picked up a name tag from the reception desk and walked in. Anticipating that I might need reinforcements, I headed straight for the bar.

Looking as though they were right from central casting, two yuppie and "waspie" looking characters—complete with blue blazers, tan pants, loafers with no socks, one of them actually wearing an ascot—approached me. I took a deep breath.

"I'm Marshall."

"William."

Shaking their hands. "Nice to meet you both, I'm Carl Cusato."

"Is that an 'I'talian name?" Marshall said.

"Yes, 'I'talian." This is not a good beginning, I thought.

"My roommate at Princeton was half 'I'talian."

"Was that the upper half or lower half?" I have to thank Groucho for that line.

"I beg your pardon." Marshall had a real sense of humor.

"Bad joke, sorry."

"Where did you go to school?" William inquired.

"I graduated from SUNY at Albany."

"Oh, is that a *public* school?"

"Not in the British sense."

"Ha, ha, you're very quick." William had such a genuine laugh.

"Where do you work?"

"I'm Assistant to the Chairman and President at Norton Simon."

There was an extended silence as if they were caught by surprise.

"Who did you know? I mean, how did you get *that* job?"

"I interviewed for it."

William turned to Marshall. "Isn't that the job that Bert Prichard was chasing?"

Turning back to me, "Bert has his MBA from Harvard. Where did you say you got yours?"

"I'm still working at it."

"You know, we got Mr. Norton Simon to show his art collection at Princeton at no charge. In fact, we even made money on the showing."

"Sounds like a deal to me. I don't think he's ever done *that* before. Must have caught him sleeping."

"By the way…" William, sensing my sarcasm, changed the subject. "Where do you summer?"

"Where do I summer…? Where I winter." *That supercilious little prick*, I thought. I wanted to say *with your mother.* "Excuse me, where's the nearest head?" I needed some air.

"Down the hallway on your left."

I couldn't wait to get out of that room. I had warmer times talking to the meat inspectors in the freezers at the Chosen Hotel in Korea. Imagine thinking they could outwit Norton. Well, at least I showed some restraint.

When I returned from the head, they were waiting for me at the door.

"Thank you for coming." They turned, and closed the door on my face.

The next morning Desch called me.

"Well, I have good news and bad news. The admissions committee and the guys that wrote letters liked you, but the younger men's committee voted against you."

"I only met two of them."

"We've had this problem before. They're full of themselves. They don't run the club, we do…the little fuckers."

Exactly my sentiment, I thought. "What do you want me to do?"

"I have set up two more meetings with the other admissions committee members. The younger men only have one vote anyway. Are you okay with that?"

"Sure, I appreciate all that you're doing."

I had the meetings, and a week later I was admitted. It made me realize that knowing the right people, regardless of the importance of the issue, is how the world turns.

I called Desch and thanked him for all his help. I said, "You know, sir, I feel like the chairman of the board who was in the hospital recovering from a heart attack when the president came to visit. The president said, "You'll be happy to know the board has passed a resolution wishing you a speeding recovery…the vote was six to five."

I paid my dues and became a member in good standing.

The great irony of all this was that Charley Buck, one of the guys that I had interviewed, was Chairman of the Baths. He was looking for people to serve on his committee. The Bath Committee set policy and was responsible for the health club in the basement. I volunteered to serve, and we met biweekly for lunch to discuss how to improve the facility.

After about a year, Charley was leaving town, and he recommended that I take over as chairman.

Being a department chairman, even though it was a volunteer position, was a big deal because it automatically made one a member of the Executive Board. The Executive Board met once a month in the club's boardroom on the tenth floor. The dress was black tie, and we sat down to a gourmet, multi-course meal complete with fine wines. After dinner, it was brandy and cigars. This was the club's center of power.

At each meeting, the committee chairman would present his report to the board. The admissions, house, squash, chess, younger men's, library, and bath committees were all represented. I had finally arrived. One year in the club…and I was sitting in the boardroom. How quaint? My buddies on the young men's committee were not overjoyed by my good fortune.

At the first meeting, I looked around and noticed that other than myself and one or two other guys, this was a very senior group. No wonder it was such an honor to be part of this monthly event. The president introduced me, and the board applauded. I was a little nervous for my first report. I wrote out what I wanted to say and memorized it. It was actually an idea that we had talked about at our committee luncheons.

I told them that the time had come to invest in the health of our members and that the finest men's club in New York should have the finest athletic facilities. Currently, the facility consisted of a pool, a sauna and steam room, a weight room with a few pulleys, and a locker room that was fifty years old. Renovation was way overdue. Surprisingly, I got their support conceptually, contingent on presenting a more complete report later. I think they liked the new blood at the table.

I met with the House Committee chairman several times over the next few weeks. He was an executive with Turner Construction. Turner was a big construction company with lots of resources. The next month I made my presentation.

I proposed new paint and carpet; a weight room with Nautilus equipment; an aerobic room with treadmills, bicycles, and a cross-country ski machine; new lockers; and a large twelve-person Jacuzzi. I found turn-of-the-century poster art for the walls and one of the original full-size prints of the famous Sutra baths in San Francisco for the entrance—all without changing the historical décor and for the bargain basement price of $250,000.

I held my breath during the silence and then applause began. They loved the idea. The money wasn't even an issue. It's good to be around rich people. After the questions and suggestions that lasted almost a half hour, I made my final request.

"We need to change the name of the baths."

"It's been called the Baths since the club opened," one member commented. I didn't realize that I was on sacred ground. I probably should have waited, but it was too late now.

"I know and I hate to tamper with tradition, but the term *baths* has evolved to connote a meeting place for gay men." The crowd grew restless.

"You mean homosexuals," one of the old men commented.

"To prevent any misunderstanding, I am proposing that we change it to the Fitness Center."

This was harder to do than getting the money approved. The discussion went back and forth. Finally, they voted and approved the money and the name change.

After the meeting, one of the more senior members came over to me.

"Congratulations and welcome to the board. It's good to have a *stem-winder* like you around."

Stem-winder? I thought. Sounds like a compliment.

35

That Dangerous Brandy at 21

One of the more exciting parts of my job at NSI was managing the corporate jet. The company owned a BAC 111. It was a twin-engine, short-to-medium range jet that was used by the airlines for routes less than 1500 miles. With the two engines mounted on the tail, it looked much like the DC9. Retrofitted for corporate use, the range was extended with larger fuel tanks and lighter loads. Instead of carrying one hundred passengers, the *Skyrunner* was configured to carry twenty-two but rarely carried more than six. The interior was decorated in leather and rich fabrics with plush over-sized seats, a meeting table, two fold-out beds, and a full galley.

Virtually every company that owned a private jet hired an aircraft management company to manage the day-to-day operations. With all the government regulations, safety requirements, and crew training, it made sense to out-source to a licensed operator.

We hired Executive Air Fleet to manage our plane, and I was the interface. EAF was a successful company operating out of Tetterboro Airport in New Jersey. Matt Wiesman, a lawyer who loved airplanes, founded the company. By the time I met Matt, he had over twenty airplanes under contract with Fortune 500 companies such as JC Penny and Met Life.

EAF handled all the details. They maintained the plane, hired and trained the crew, and provided a detailed budget on operating expenses.

My job was to ensure that things went smoothly. In that regard, Matt and I met regularly and eventually became friends.

Our favorite spot for dinner was the 21 Club, the former speakeasy on West 52nd Street. It was Mahoney's favorite hangout as well as that of many of Matt's clients. We both knew Jack Kriendler, one of the original founders, and were always given a good table.

One night, after a few martinis and steak dinner, we settled back for cigars and brandy. As we mellowed, we began talking about the idea of starting a premium class airline. First-class service had deteriorated since deregulation, and airports were congested and noisy.

Our thought was to create a commercial airline product unlike anything on the market. We'd offer privacy, security, and an environment conducive to productivity. We would lease Boeing 727s, retrofit the interior to seat 34 rather than 128, and add long-range fuel tanks. We wanted to create a club-like atmosphere for the discriminating traveler. We would start small with two flights a day from New York to Los Angeles and from New York to Houston. Houston was a hot, rich city in those days. As the brandies continued, we became more and more enamored with the idea.

As weeks progressed, we continued to develop the idea. Matt took a three-month leave to attend Harvard's Advanced Management program. When he returned, he was even more excited about starting a new company. I had worked for NSI for more than five years and was ready to take on a new challenge.

EAF would provide the funds during the planning stage. The company had the operational capabilities and personnel to handle the plane and all the required regulations. I would be responsible for marketing and sales. It seemed like a slam-dunk. With the aircraft management reputation and all the corporate contacts of EAF, raising money shouldn't have been a problem.

We hired Skaden Arps, the prestigious New York Law firm as our lawyers, and First Boston, the investment-banking firm, as our bankers. All we needed to do was write a business plan, and we'd raise the money and start operations.

I met with Mahoney and told him of my idea. He was supportive but cautious. He said that I was taking a big chance leaving the company, but he would help out any way he could. He generously gave me six months' severance with health benefits.

I went home to tell my wife. She wasn't too excited. In fact, she was petrified of the risk. I spent a week wearing her down. Finally, she reluctantly agreed.

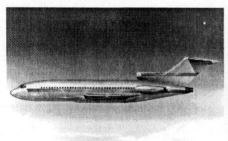

AirCore 727

AirCore 34 seat config

AirCore Conference

AirCore Lounge

I found offices on Third Avenue and hired a secretary. We settled on the name *AirCore Aviation* and began working out the logistics. Matt was possessed with writing a great business plan. Personally, I just wanted to buy some planes and get started.

The logistics of an airline, even one as small as ours, was mind-boggling. The marketing was the easiest part. We had to secure gate space in the three cities, deal with caterers, develop hiring policies, develop maintenance manuals, secure FAA approvals, and, of course, develop several years of believable financial forecasts.

We developed fancy four-color brochures and contacted several Fortune 500 companies to test their reaction. Their response was encouraging. We were providing all the benefits of private jet travel only on a scheduled basis and for a fraction of owning a plane.

I traveled regularly to L.A. and Houston to arrange for gate space and develop relationships with limo operators. AirCore was a door-to-door service. We'd pick up the passengers and drop them off at their final destination. With only thirty-four spacious seats it was truly "above-the-crowd service." The food service was equivalent to a fine restaurant.

I was getting more excited about success as the days progressed. With only a moderate degree of success I would finally be financially independent. In my dreams, I had already picked out the color of my Porsche.

Unfortunately, what I thought would take six months had taken almost two years. For two years, I was totally immersed and possessed with making this venture happen. We had a business plan the size of the New York City telephone book and I was running out of money.

The most serious thing that occurred, and something that I neglected to notice, was that between 1978 and 1980 interest rates had risen to the highest level in history. By the end of the Carter administration, interest grew beyond 20 percent. The airline industry had lost millions. While I was out planning and marketing, the picture for raising money for a start-up airline was getting darker and darker. Finally, in a meeting with our bankers, they announced that the *investment window had closed*. I was crushed. I had made two classic monumental mistakes—*I fell in love with an idea and I used my own money*. They recommended that *we put it aside for a year or two*.

I couldn't put it aside. I had run out of money. It was bad enough that my dream of being on the cover of Forbes had disappeared. The fact that I had gone into debt and put my family's security at risk was devastating.

People talk about how the ebbs in life build character, but until it happens it is hard to understand how frightening it can be. I had fallen in love with an idea and, like most people in love, I lost all my common sense. My career up to this point had been effortless. I had succeeded without really trying. Now it was different. I was isolated. I didn't have a job from which to leverage. Childishly, I was embarrassed. I had bragged how great my plans were to everyone I knew. Now that I had failed, it was hard facing them. I couldn't focus.

I had a home in Greenwich, a BMW in the driveway, a wife and two young children to feed, clothe, and educate. I was in a funk for a couple of months. I was scared. I had thrown away great security for a dream, and now the dream had suddenly disappeared.

One day I was walking along the beach in my town, and it occurred to me that I was worth more dead than alive. As that thought crossed my mind, it was as though I was spiritually slapped. I finally realized that I had to be a man, pick myself up, and start again.

The next day I was at the club copying and mailing out my résumé. I took a break and went down to the fitness center for a steam. There, I started talking to one of the club board members, Nelson. Nelson had retired from a big job in insurance and now was doing deals. He knew about my venture, and I told him what happened. He asked if I were interested in doing some consulting. He was about to invest in a technology company in California and wanted to know if I would go out and evaluate it. The company needed a few million and offered him a bunch of stock and two board seats. He needed to know if the technology was real. Although I knew absolutely nothing about geographic database management systems, I jumped at the opportunity. Little did Nelson know how much I needed the work. It was a two-month retainer, a chance to make some immediate cash, and pay some bills.

When I got home, I told my wife, and she cried from relief. I didn't realize how emotionally distraught she had been, and how much of a strain it had put on our relationship. The airline was the equivalent of a mistress. It drained my time and all my emotions. To this day, I still carry the guilt of putting her and the kids though the ordeal.

I flew to Newport Beach, California and began a new career in consulting and crisis management. This began a phase in my life where I would learn more about the business of business in one year than I had in the past fifteen.

Before I leave the subject of the failed airline, I must admit that although I was beginning to pick up the pieces of my life, the scars never really disappeared. Not only did it take me nearly a decade to pay off my debts, but like the high diver who hits the diving board, I was never quite as fearless. I also never truly recovered from the guilt of jeopardizing my family's welfare. I forgot that poor kids don't have nets. The secret I carry is that I have been looking down ever since.

36

Renaissance and the West

When you have been set back as badly as I had, your sense of invulnerability evaporates, and mine certainly had. Making matters worse, I had pulled the rug out from under myself. I had no one to blame but me. Why did I fail? I failed because I had an entrepreneurial spirit but not the entrepreneurial skills. I knew how to survive in an established company like American Airlines, but knew nothing about how to bring an idea to the marketplace. Starting a company is a different culture, with different skills and levels of risk. I wasn't prepared for the land mines. Luckily, I was in my mid-thirties and had plenty of time to learn it the right way. I needed new skills and a new start.

Newport Beach was a great place to re-energize. It was bright, clean, and uncongested. The assignment lasted only a few months, but this time I was outside *looking in* at a new venture rather than the other way around. I could see they were making the same mistakes that I had made. I could have stayed and helped them, but I found out that their technology, which was the basis of the enterprise and investment, was suspect. I returned to New York and recommended against the investment. Nelson was happy; unfortunately, the company in California was not.

One exception was Dr. Rick, one of the West Coast investor/directors. He called me after I returned to New York. He said he liked my report and wished that I had worked with him before he invested.

My business education was about to intensify. Instead of continuing in the proper club-like world of the Fortune 500, I was now thrown into the new wild and freewheeling world of startups and penny stocks.

Dr. Rick was a medical doctor and a lawyer, but practiced neither. He was a gambler, a big game hunter, and an entrepreneur, all of which he practiced actively. He had been married several times and was currently connubially connected to a pretty young thing in her twenties. A year passed when I received a call from him about another venture.

By that time, I had started a company called *Renaissance Management* to consult and handle crisis management. I had completed projects in fast food, trade publishing, and dental equipment. This was another opportunity to go West.

There are two principal ways of taking a company public. One is the traditional method of hiring underwriters and investment bankers to execute an IPO (initial public offering). This way is costly and you risk not selling enough, or getting your price for the shares.

The other less-costly, back-door method is to find an inactive public company called a *shell* and merge it with an ongoing private company. You file a Form 10 with the SEC. The interests are, in effect, pooled and a reverse merger is performed. The inactive stock is then activated. It usually takes a few brokers to make the market.

In the treasury box of the shell company is generally a pile of stock; some of it is lettered or restricted and the other is tradable. The initial tradable stock usually goes to the early investors and the brokers who are making the market. The lettered stock is generally given to the management or used for acquisition.

Lettered stock generally can't be sold for two years. This was designed to keep the management and the brokers honest. Without restrictions, the price of the stock could be run up artificially, leaving the unconnected investor holding the bag. This is the world of the penny stock market.

The company Rick spoke of was one of these reverse merger public companies. Investor/bankers found a reasonable healthy private company that made components for the manufactured housing market (mobile homes). They promised the owner a way of going public and getting rich. Using restricted treasury stock, they began acquiring other small private companies. By the time I arrived, it was a small conglomerate. The stock had not made an index yet but was closely traded on the pink sheets by a broker in Chicago and one in Irvine, California.

Their pitch to the entrepreneurial owners they acquired was that they would handle the financials, i.e., receivables, payables, and bank relationships plus all stockholder and SEC issues, while allowing the owners to focus on sales and marketing. They gave them an overly generous amount of company stock for their companies that was valued at a dollar (artificially by the market makers) and guaranteed $3 per share in two years. Greed is a great aphrodisiac.

This was the wild-west world of the company that I was retained to evaluate. The truth was that Dr. Rick wanted someone in management to protect his interest. The chairman/president was a very charming, believable guy and was responsible for the acquisitions.

He acquired an after-market auto wheel company, an auto polish and wax company, a laser entertainment company, a chemical repacking company, and a company that made fake hardwood siding for mobile homes. Each operating company directed its sales receipts to the corporate office. The corporate office would pay all expenses and collect all receivables. Sounds logical and you could easily see how attractive it would be to the small businessman who was struggling to grow his company.

When I first arrived, I was paid by Dr. Rick and was living at his house in Laguna Beach. He introduced me to the company as his board representative. It was initially a little awkward, but I quickly developed a rapport with the president. He convinced me how devoted he was to making the venture work, but he needed talented people to help him.

I was impressed with how clever he was at putting the company together. With less than a $100,000 investment, he had acquired several million dollars in assets—all perfectly legal and all apparently in the open. Unfortunately, the company's internal financial systems were weak as was the operational reporting, but I attributed that to lack of staff and time.

I was a little surprised when the next week he offered me a generous employment contract. It was a three-year contract for $100K plus a car and expenses for airline trips back home and to cover my living costs. In addition, I would receive 500,000 shares of restricted stock. I was flattered.

They leased an apartment for me at Promontory Point in Newport Beach. It was an upscale apartment complex not far from the beach. A BMW was leased and I was given the title Executive Vice President Operations.

My plan was to commute biweekly to Connecticut until school ended for the kids, and then move the family out. It was stressful for my wife and me, but it appeared to be an excellent opportunity to get back on our feet financially.

Everything seemed to be going well for the first few months. The accounting system was getting better. Everyone was getting paid. About two months into the assignment, the operating presidents started coming to me complaining that their bills were getting paid late and then weren't getting paid at all. When I inquired, I was told it was cash flow and difficulty in collecting receivables as well as a number of one-time start-up expenses. As a CPA, the president managed the financial operations personally. Soon, I was being sent out on exploratory meetings with potential new acquisitions.

When I overheard the president talk about paying off one of the company presidents by selling restricted stock, I knew there was a problem. When I confronted him with the issue, I was accused of being disloyal and suddenly I was being ignored.

Finally, I resigned and negotiated my contract. The operating presidents came to me for help. They had sold their companies for a dream and now they were faced with the loss of everything. I recommended they immediately seek counsel. I was able to get three months' severance. I knew I was lucky to get that so I didn't fight it.

As it turned out, the president and his market makers were embezzling from the company. Instead of paying the bills, they were paying themselves huge sums. I headed back to New York. Since the board never approved my position, I was not officially an officer and did not have a fiduciary responsibility for the acts of the president. The president and his gang continued running the company for another year, but were finally charged by the SEC. Dr. Rick lost a little money, but then disappeared. Most of the operating companies were eventually returned to their original owners. It was an outstanding idea that could have been extremely successful if the principals weren't greedy and dishonest.

I learned that things too good to be true, usually are. I was sorry that it didn't work out, but I am much smarter for the experience.

37

A Collection of Originals

The Ashkenazy brothers emigrated to the U.S. from France in the late fifties. They moved to France before the war to escape the Nazi threat in Poland. Their father worked for the government helping with the Polish reconstruction. They were a business-oriented family, and soon after their arrival they opened a chicken ranch while investing in real estate.

By the late seventies, they owned a number of apartment buildings in West Hollywood and Beverly Hills. Severyn, the younger of the two sons, began converting the apartment houses into luxury suite hotels and, in some circles, is credited with creating the all-suite hotel concept. His hotel company was known as *The L'Ermitage Group*. The older brother, Arnold, began expanding the art collection that the family had brought with them from Europe.

Shortly before I left my job in Newport Beach, I sent out a stack of résumés to headhunters. The day before I was leaving to return home, one of the headhunters called about an unusual opportunity in the hotel business. L'Ermitage Hotels was headed for Chapter 11 and needed someone to reinvigorate the company. I met Severyn the morning of my flight back East. We hit it off immediately. He told me that he needed someone to head up his sales and marketing organization.

There were eight all-suite properties located in a ten-block radius in fashionable West Hollywood and Beverly Hills. He felt that he had an excellent product and was concerned that his occupancy was so low. I gave him a few ideas, and he provided a limo to the airport for my trip home.

When I got home, I told my wife, Robin, about what had happened in Newport. I could see that the stress of my being away plus the added stress of our inconsistent income was getting to her. I didn't have another assignment and the money was still tight. I was still paying down some of the debt that I accumulated from the airline venture.

When Ashkenazy called the next week, I received his offer with mixed feelings. We were relieved about the money, but uncomfortable about the thought of my being away again with Robin raising the two kids alone. Ashley was ten, and Damon was twelve.

Ashkenazy's offer was generous but temporary. It would be a three-month assignment. I would work fourteen days and return home for six. After three months, my position would be reviewed and a contract written if we were compatible. Given my situation, I didn't have much choice.

The following Sunday I flew back to L.A. and moved into the L'Ermitage Hotel on Burton Way in Beverly Hills.

As I sat in my office the next day, I felt good about being back in a more stable environment. Even though the company was not in good shape, it had hard-working people and excellent products.

The eight hotels employed over 800 people, many of them actors—after all, this was L.A. Severyn was the company's greatest asset and its greatest liability. Coming from an upper-class European background, he was highly literate in the arts and music. He understood the etiquette of his class and knew fine foods and wines. His hotels were a reflection of that sophistication. His family collected art while in Europe, and his brother, Arnold, maintained and expanded the collection after they emigrated. The hotels were filled with over 1500 pieces of original art, some of which were very valuable. The hotels were named after artists liked Duffy, Valadon, and Mondrian, or had French names like L'Ermitage, Bel Age, Le Parc, and Le Rive.

The hotels with the exception of the Bel Age were all converted apartment houses. This is how the all-suite concept evolved. Every room had a large sitting area, separate from the bedroom. In addition, Severyn was the first to put a variety of amenities in the bathrooms like perfumes, skin care products, shampoos, and exotic soaps.

The L'Ermitage was the flagship of the group. Located on Burton Way, in a residential section of Beverly Hills, it was a hideout for celebrities. It had a small, intimate lobby with walls covered in hardwoods. For the very private, there was an underground parking lot entrance so they could enter and leave the hotel without being seen. Next to the hotel was a two-story convent-looking building with twelve rooms that was to be used for servants who were traveling with their employers. The basic room was a split-level suite with a living room and bedroom. On the roof, there was the pool and a private Jacuzzi, plus private cabanas for sunbathing.

The only restaurant was the Café Russé, which was located on the top floor and, because of zoning restrictions, was only open to the hotel guests. As an indication of his genius, Severyn turned the restaurant and pool area into a club with part of the proceeds going to UCLA. This allowed him access to the local market, and provided tax advantages. It was brilliant. We had free concerts and literary readings for the members, most of which were provided with the help of UCLA. The restaurant business grew, as did its unique reputation. An example of its elegance was that happy hour consisted of free caviar, and a live classical guitarist.

If it were possible to build a hotel experience that was slightly above the heads of the market, it was L'Ermitage. From a marketing perspective, the problem was awareness. Each hotel was being marketed individually with it own salespeople and reservation department.

My first act was to hire an advertising agency and develop a campaign. Next, I consolidated the sales and reservations functions and began to redesign the sales materials. I presented a business plan to the board with a new corporate logo and advertising campaign. It was unanimously approved. A week later, I was offered an employment contract almost two months sooner than the planned review period. Stirring things up quickly was something I thoroughly enjoyed.

The new campaign was called "A Collection of Originals." It played off the uniqueness of the properties and their artistic flavor. We picked famous artists and had the billboard people reproduce their art on billboards across the Westside of Los Angeles. For example, the Mondrian billboard had a reproduction of Piet Mondrian's *Broadway Boogie Woogie,* with copy that simply said "Mondrian Hotel, A Collection of Originals, West Hollywood."

With a great campaign and a well-thought-out marketing strategy, I was left with only one problem: I had no money to advertise. Luckily, Severyn was a great believer in barter—the age-old practice of trading goods and services.

In one year, we bartered over $4 million in ad space. We were in all the major business and consumer publications with full-page spreads. We had eight billboards that rotated every thirty days throughout L.A.'s Westside. Our TV exposure was mainly game shows where the prize would be a stay at one of our properties. We developed preferred guest programs similar to the frequent-flyer programs of today.

To build local interest, I hired Skip E. Lowe, a local entertainment industry gadfly, to host "Catch a Rising Star." Every Sunday night, singers, musicians, and comics could showcase their talents at the Mondrian. They would bring their friends and relatives to watch them perform. Since we only paid Skip, our costs were negligible, while it tripled our restaurant and bar business.

Meanwhile, I was still commuting. Finally, the family decided that we'd move at the end of the school year. For almost eight months, I commuted or they came out for long weekends. In June, we sold our house in Cos Cob, moved to California, and found a house in the Palisades.

Occupancy and average rate steadily grew. We still had problem with Le Petite L'Ermitage, which was the small building next to L'Ermitage that was supposed to be used for servants of the rich. The occupancy was a miserable 10 percent or about one room per night.

We got the idea to convert it to a post-surgical cosmetic retreat. It was to be used for the first few days of recovery for those having had surgery. It had round-the-clock nurses and a limo directly from the out-patient operating room to the subterranean private entrance. We produced a brochure and had a reception for the local plastic surgeons and their staffs. It was an immediate success. Occupancy went up to 90 percent and the average rate went from $60 to $400.

This was now 1988, and the average rate for hotel rooms even at the luxurious properties was no more than $150 per night. The chain's occupancy grew to over 70 percent with an average rate of nearly $160.

What had started as a three-month assignment lasted three years. In spite of the improved conditions, the hotels, because they were so highly leveraged, were still financially pressured. Severyn's liability was that he was very hard on his people and we were constantly going through managers.

We fought regularly but it was always constructive. Finally, I convinced him to give a bonus to the Sales Department if we reached a certain quota. The quota was reached and the bonus didn't materialize. At the time, I had about fifteen salespeople reporting to me and I had promised them the bonus. Severyn and I argued over whether repeat customers counted toward the quota. My argument was that in the service business, repeat customers were the only definition of success. I knew that he couldn't argue that point. Still, the financial pressures took their toll on the company and our relationship. Although it was on a friendly basis, we parted company and I went on to my next venture. Two years later, all the properties were sold off to different hotel operators, and Severyn moved to Russia to begin development there.

For me, another great adventure had ended.

38

An Apple for the Educated

Staring at computer screens
In my faded, baggy jeans
Running up more phone bills for my dad

Hard drive forty megabytes
Stores the programs that I write
Running up more phone bills for my dad

Now my schoolwork has to wait
For the software I'll create
Running up more phone bills for my dad

Sold the program to Big Blue
Now the bread is coming through
Earning more than phone bills for my dad

—*Damon Cusato*—*Who's Who among High School*
    Writers—*LAUSD 1989*

I received several months of severance so getting relocated was important but not critical. I restarted Renaissance Management and almost immediately I found a consulting assignment in Northern California. Sometimes things happen when you're not looking.

I liked the idea of spending more time with the family. Damon and Ashley were both in high school, and it was important for me to be around. They were both competitive swimmers, so we spent most weekends at swim meets. Since swimmers only swim three or four events, it was only five to ten minutes of swimming excitement and six to eight hours of waiting—creating lots of time to bond. One day my daughter asked if I would sell some ads in their swim program. It helped support the team and gave her a chance to win some prizes.

Here is another example of unplanned opportunity changing the direction of life. Early one Friday morning, I made a list of businesses in the area and their locations. The ads were so inexpensive that it was hard for a business owner to say no, especially when it involved a non-profit enterprise for kids.

As I was walking down Santa Monica Boulevard, I passed the Micro-Age store. A few weeks before, I had purchased an Apple computer for Damon. The owner, Henry, a very pleasant guy, helped me out, and we had fun negotiating the price.

As I walked in the store, he remembered me. Apple was big in education, and as a dealer, he had promotional money called *Apple dollars* specifically to be used to promote the brand. He bought a full-page ad on the back page. We talked about my consulting business and some of my business experiences.

Personal computers were just beginning to take off, and the only people with the skills to sell them were young guys who as teens taught each other how to assemble, program, and use them. The average age of Henry's staff was early twenties. His problem was that they had the computer literacy, but lacked sales and business skills. He asked if I could help out for a few weeks in developing a program to make his salespeople more effective.

As it developed, I had two assignments pending but nothing signed. I told him that my computer skills were nonexistent and I could barely turn one on. He said that was not a problem. We agreed on a one-month retainer, and I started the following Monday.

The first few days I sat with a trainer to learn the basic concepts and language of the personal computer. I then spent another day in the repair shop watching the technicians assemble and disassemble the boxes. It was like learning a new language: hard drives, memory SIMMs and DIMMs, bits and bytes, interfaces, buses, and processors, and that was just the hardware. Once I got beyond the language, it was easier than I imagined. The hardest thing about a computer is deciding to learn to use one. Once you sit down and learn to turn it on, much of the mystery disappears.

The greatest development in software was the graphic user interface, GUI (gooie). The use of icons and simple pull-down menus quickly made the use of word processing and spreadsheet programs approachable to the average person. Much of the complicated syntax and protocols needed to operate these programs had disappeared with the introduction of Apple's Macintosh software and Microsoft's Windows. Ironically, these two companies and their leaders became sinfully rich by using a technology stolen from Xerox.

I began making sales calls with each of the reps, covering a variety of market segments. The day I spent with the rep who handled the school districts, we called on the purchasing director for L.A. County. Bob had the reputation of being very tough with vendors and difficult to see. He spent the first fifteen minutes telling us why we shouldn't do business with him. He then spent the next five minutes inquiring about my background. I noticed a brochure on his desk for a multilevel marketing type product like an Amway. I ignored everything about selling computers or doing business with the county and began to talk about the pros and cons of MLM.

Multilevel marketing (also called network marketing) is a form of direct sales in which independent distributors sell products, usually in their customers' homes or by telephone. In theory, distributors can make money not only from their own sales but also from those of the people they recruit.

Vitamins, herbs, homeopathic remedies, weight-loss powders, or other health-related products make up the majority of these companies. For a small investment, usually less than $100, you can become a distributor. The idea is to recruit others and you build what is called a "*down line*." The larger the *down line* (assuming they are active), the more money made. Statistically about 1 percent is successful, another 5 percent make a modest living, and over 90 percent fail.

Bob was sucked into one of these schemes and was fascinated with the concept. While I was in Newport, I had become friends with the founder of one these MLM companies. He eventually shared a ton of information on the subtleties of the business, while trying hard to recruit me. As much as I liked him, he had a shady quality and I kept my business interests separate from our socializing.

My conversation with Bob eventually turned into lunch, and it was apparent that we were becoming friends. Before we left, he asked if we were interested in replying to an RFP (request for proposal) to handle his Apple Computer Products. My experience in writing business plans paid off. I responded with a document that was worthy of the boardroom. We were granted the contract and suddenly Henry's business increased by $3 million.

I only had one week left on my agreement with MicroAge. Henry and I went out to dinner to celebrate and to talk about the future. Obviously, the county contract would be jeopardized if I left. We agreed on six months with a retainer, bonus, and lease car.

It was hard to imagine that doing a simple favor for my daughter would result in changing my career.

As I began contracting school districts, Apple called Henry and asked him to stop me from signing additional contracts. Apple computer was dominant in education with more than a 60 percent market share. They were redefining their marketing tactics. They decided to divide up the sales territories and assign them to certified resellers on an exclusive basis. In exchange for our cooperation, Apple offered to include us in the program. As a result, we were given one-sixth of Southern California or approximately $6 million in incremental business. My career had now made another turn!

Since starting in 1990, computer technology not only in education but in general grew at an incredible rate. At forty-five, I was already an old man in industry terms. I liked the business. I liked the idea of learning, and I felt good about working with school districts. These were all the right ingredients for success.

My success in the computer business was not a result of my developing extraordinary technology skills, but that I translated well. "Techies" or "propeller heads," in most cases because of their youth and immaturity, tried to intimidate by showing off their knowledge by using obscure acronyms, and acting annoyed by the listener's technical ignorance. This abrupt, elitist attitude turned off many potential buyers and users.

The decision to integrate technology into the school curriculum quickly changed from an elective skill to part of the mainstream learning process. School administrators were soon being judged on how well the district managed this integration process. Millions were being spent and no one wanted to make a mistake, or look stupid. I recognized early that making these decisions as painless as possible was the key to success. Using plain English to explain the technology and simple examples to clarify concepts not only was endearing to the school management, but also built a trust that has lasted over a decade

Working with technology for the past fifteen years has been exciting. During that time, I have represented virtually all the major hardware manufacturers and software publishers and worked with over thirty school districts selling hardware, software, and building network infrastructure. I finally opened my own business and soon became one of the largest systems integrators working the K-12 market in California.

My children are grown, successful, and visit regularly. My daughter, in spite of her degree in finance, chose to become an actor. She is still struggling but loves what she is doing. My son has developed extraordinary computer skills, holds a software patent, and is currently raising capital for a new venture with some very leading-edge technology. My wife and I live quietly in Malibu.

It has been a great trip!

Epilogue

Warning!
Everyone Hates This Chapter.

I wrote this book not only to entertain and hopefully provide a few good laughs, but also to give my children and friends a special view of who I am. Most of all, I wanted to show that an ordinary guy with few resources can have some extraordinary experiences. Life is a wonderful journey, and it is *not* a crime to enjoy it.

In this final chapter, I wanted to share some of the lessons that I have learned. Unfortunately, everyone who has read the chapter hates it. I am told that I am being pretentious because regular guys don't give advice, and because this bullshit appears in a variety of sophomoric, self-help books. So in the spirit of compromise, and in response to my friends who were kind enough to express their constructive opinion, I have chosen to leave it in.

Now, before the sophisticates around me get the vapors, allow me admit these are not earth-shaking concepts, only things that I believe are good to know. If you know this stuff already, end the book here. If you don't, who knows, it might be helpful, read on.

- So many young people worry that they don't have a specific plan—they don't know what they want to be or what they should be doing. Don't panic. I submit that by just being **open**

to new ideas and realizing that change is inevitable, things will happen. Like the lottery, you have to be in it to win it.

- We all try to plan, but unless you're from a highly structured medical, legal, or business family where your goals are defined on your behalf, or you're lucky enough to fall in love with an idea for a career early in life, all you can do is to **prepare for opportunity** and when it happens, **hope that you can recognize it**.

- Just as the world physically turns, things that affect our lives are constantly moving around and changing. The trick is to recognize the **movement** and move with it. **Trust it**, let it enhance your energy. Like the martial artist who combines the energy of his opponent to leverage his own strength, try to combine the energy that surrounds you with your own.

- **Fears and insecurities are your most powerful adversaries**. They cripple, drain energy, and blind us from the light that directs us down the path of opportunity. Most importantly, they prevent us from growing and force us to seek shelter in the world of inaction. Try to face your fears as soon as you recognize what they are. Control them before they control you. As for insecurity, here are a few tricks:

  1. Replace your negative thoughts immediately with positive ones. For example, I'm healthy. I'm good looking. It's a beautiful day. My favorite is "Be a man, you pussy, and fight."

  2. Replace the negative thoughts with a more negative thought. For example, my entire family just died in a plane crash. I have an incurable disease with only a week to live. My dog died. By comparison, your current problems will be laughable.

We all have these fears and anxieties. Those who control them usually win and those who don't lose.

- **Play to win.** Be an intellectual and emotional entrepreneur. Most people around you are living in fear and desperation. They live their lives like a bureaucrat views his job—*playing not to lose.* Think of it this way. An entrepreneur goes to the racetrack and puts his money on the horse to win, while the bureaucrat goes to the racetrack and puts his money on the horse to win, place and show, then runs back to the clubhouse, gets on his knees, and prays that the race doesn't run at all!

- **Pick your fights.** Inequities and injustices are part of life. Sometimes it happens to you and sometime it happens around you. If you choose to fight, you must decide if the fruits of the win are worth the risk of the fight. Make sure the win has substance. It should never be emotional and rarely personal. I remember watching a street fight where one of the fighters was getting beaten to a pulp. The guy who was winning either got tired or lost interest. He finally stopped and said, "Okay, I've had enough, you win." He then walked away. The beaten guy with his face black, blue, and bloody came over to me and said, "Well, I showed him." He was actually serious.

- **Try to find the win-win whenever possible.** Whether it's a business venture, a love affair or a friendship, it rarely works unless both parties feel that they have acquired something positive and/or meaningful. The combined energy produced creates good karma.

- **There are no free lunches.** Unless you've won the lottery or have fallen into a room full of deranged philanthropists, everything has a cost. It may not be upfront or apparent, but it is there. Simply be guarded when something too good to be true is offered—because it always is.

- **You're never a victim.** People are too selfish, too self-absorbed, too concerned with their own comforts to waste time victimizing others. You are the only one who can make you a victim. If you feel you're being treated unfairly, figure a way to fix it or leave. Accept your failures as part of your learning experience.

• **The only thing worse than failing is not trying**. The only ones who don't experience failure are those who never try anything. It's okay to fail. It has happened to virtually every successful person on the planet. It is part of the growth process. There is nothing more pathetic than someone nearing the end of his or her life pre-occupied with the "should'ves" or "could'ves" of the past.

• **Don't fall in love with anything but another person.** When it comes to business or any meaningful project, emotionalism is generally inefficient and illogical. If I had not fallen in love with my airline venture, I would have seen the reality, made changes to succeed, or cut my losses sooner. The inefficiency of love is best practiced on people. True love is worth the land mines.

• **Intimacy is not sex. It is trust**. Once broken, it is nearly impossible to fix. Like glass, you will always see the cracks. Be careful with the one or ones you love.

• **Marriage should be forever,** or at least that should be your intention going in. If it isn't your intention, it will surely fail. Here are some basic rules for success:

Roots. Check the family. Acorns don't fall far from the tree. Nut trees produce nuts. Fruit trees produce fruit. The chances are that what has happened will likely repeat itself.

Happiness. You can create happy events, but for the long term, true sustained happiness is only self-generated. Neediness is an incurable disease that spreads and eventually suffocates everything in its path. If you sense neediness, run for the hills.

Space. You must agree that there is to be your space, her space, and shared space. Uncontrolled togetherness eventually produces uncontrolled screaming.

Don't have kids unless you are prepared for a lifetime of unselfishness. They are not toys, trophies, or hobbies. They are an extension of your existence that needs teaching, nurturing, protecting, and unrequited love.

The responsibility is forever. Be prepared.

Communication should never be totally open. It should be on a need-to-know or on a whether-it-will-enhance-the-relationship basis. I am not advocating lying, just that from a practical perspective everything need not or should not necessarily be shared. Details on past intimacies, aesthetic opinions on the defects of your mate, or the quality of the neighbor's derriere are subjects best avoided.

Two rules on marriage from Uncle Mustacche. On the day of my wedding, my uncle was too ill to attend. My mother insisted that I visit him out of respect and to get the envelope with the $10 wedding gift. As we sat in his living room drinking anisette from glasses previously filled with Welch's grape jam, he shared two important principles for a successful marriage. The first was **"never do woman's work,"** including cooking, cleaning, ironing, etc. I did. He was right. I am sorry for not following his advice. If a woman knows you can do something, she will make sure that you do. It is best to remain stupid and be catered to.

Uncle Mustacche and Mary

His second principle was **"Deny it,"** which he explained in this way:

"Letsa say you ina bed with a your *godmadre*, and you wifea comes home. She says, 'What are you a doing in a bed with that woman?'

"You say, '*aspettare un momento!*'

"You turna to your *godmadre* and tell her to go home. Once she has a left, you turn to your wife and ask, 'What was your question?'

"She says, 'What were you doing in bed with that woman?'

"You calmly say, 'What woman?'"

Mustacche had great advice, maybe not so good timing.

Finally, **laugh as often as you can, and at yourself when you can.** It is not only good for your health, but it is also one of the greater aphrodisiacs in existence. It clears your mind and cleanses your body.

I hope that I have made you smile and think just a little.

THE END

978-0-595-38960-5
0-595-38960-0

Printed in the United States
51610LVS00003B/220-252

9 780595 389605